C000002797

THE
NOTTS COUNTY
MISCELLANY

DAVID CLAYTON

The History Press

For Jay-Jay, Bo and Chrissie
All my love, Daddy xxxx

First published 2010

The History Press
The Mill, Brimscombe Port
Stroud, Gloucestershire, GL5 2QG
www.thehistorypress.co.uk

© David Clayton, 2010

The right of The Author to be identified as the Author
of this work has been asserted in accordance with the
Copyrights, Designs and Patents Act 1988.

All rights reserved. No part of this book may be reprinted
or reproduced or utilised in any form or by any electronic,
mechanical or other means, now known or hereafter invented,
including photocopying and recording, or in any information
storage or retrieval system, without the permission in writing
from the Publishers.

British Library Cataloguing in Publication Data.
A catalogue record for this book is available from the British
Library.

ISBN 978 0 7524 5877 9

Typesetting and origination by The History Press
Printed in Great Britain
Manufacturing managed by Jellyfish Print Solutions Ltd

AUTHOR'S
ACKNOWLEDGEMENTS

Because of the 'Pies' lack of success over the years, this wasn't the easiest project to research, but I hope I've got in everything of relevance. Despite the hard work, I really enjoyed putting this book together and it brought back a lot of happy memories for me. As a kid my favourite Subbuteo players were a one-armed Les Bradd (in Arsenal colours – don't ask), Paul Hooks, a yellow and green footballer pen-top named Steve Carter and a red and black striped Ray O'Brien – the penalty expert, of course! It made up for not really having the money to go and watch County and that Subbuteo team were my Notts County – even if the cat sometimes did a poor impersonation of the Scotland supporters invading the Wembley pitch and breaking the nets on occasion. To write about some of those same players was a pleasure and, when I'm next in the attic, I might just dust down that old biscuit tin and see how the lads are getting on!

The odd thing is, things almost came full circle for me when Peter Trembling offered me the job of a media jack-of-all-trades as content editor for the club website and responsibility for the match day programme. I had grand plans of giving County fans the best of everything, including a club magazine, too, but a communications guru was then employed and I was advised things were happening behind the scenes that meant it was not the best time to start at Meadow Lane and for one reason or another, I never became an employee of Notts County Football Club. I think it would have been good, but knowing how things turned out, it was perhaps for the best at the time. I should have known it wasn't to be when Sol Campbell quit the 'Pies on the day of my original interview!

As for the actual writing of this book, I really hope you like it. For the people who made it possible, I'll keep this fairly brief. Love and respect (as they say on the streets) to my wife Sarah and my three incredibly beautiful children Harry, Jaime and Chrissie for putting up with my anxieties as the deadline approached and swiftly passed. I love you all and promise to make up the lost hours. Thanks also to Michelle Tilling, my long-suffering editor at The History Press.

That's pretty much it for this one as most of the hard work was done by Yours Truly – for facts and figures from elsewhere, thanks as well to Paul Edgar and his excellent resource site of facts and figures – 'You Pies' – at www.youpies.co.uk.

To Tony Brown, Paul Wain and Keith Warsop, thanks too. For the rest, the ones who were maybe unaccredited here and there, thank you for all your hard work and for making available for others to study and learn from – you know who you are.

David Clayton, 2010

THE A TO Z OF COUNTY

John Abthorpe, who played five games and scored three goals during the 1955/56 season for County, has the honour of sitting atop the alphabetical list of players who have represented the club. Last in the list is – hardly surprisingly – Ruben Zadkovich – who made just nine starts between 2004 and 2006.

ALL 4 ONE

County's highest scoring draw has occurred on three different occasions and each time the venue has been Meadow Lane – read into that what you will. In January 1954 the Magpies drew 4–4 with Halifax Town, while in August 1987 County drew 4–4 with Wigan Athletic – and that was the opening day of the season and was a game that was followed by a 5–3 win at York City (16 goals in the first two games, wow!) The last 4–4 draw was in November 1999 when Bristol City headed south with a useful point and the knowledge they'd just taken part in an eight-goal thriller.

ANY OLD IRE?

The fantastically named Albert Iremonger is the oldest player to represent Notts County Football Club on the field of play. Albert was just a month shy of his 42nd birthday when he went in goal against Huddersfield Town during a 4–2 win at Meadow Lane – it was his 601st appearance for the club and the end of a long, distinguished career with the Magpies. It will come as no surprise to learn he is also the club's record appearance holder, too.

WHAT'S IN A NAME?

Of all the surnames of players who have played for Notts County, Smith is the most common with nine. Second is the name Brown and Robinson with seven each while Jones, Russell and White each have four. There are a dozen surnames that have three representatives in total – here is the full list:

9	Smith
7	Brown
7	Robinson
4	Jones
4	Russell
4	White
3	Watson
3	Wilson
3	Stone
3	Richardson
3	Richards
3	Murphy
3	Johnson
3	Jackson
3	Fairclough
3	Chapman
3	Butler
3	Williams

BOMBS AWAY

An air raid on 8 May 1941 scored a direct hit on the Meadow Lane pitch, but spared the stands and terracing. A couple of huge craters rendered the surface unplayable to the extent that no football was played on the pitch whatsoever during the 1941/42 wartime season – a completely blank year in the club's football calendar. This was a rare occurrence anywhere in world football for a professional side, even during wartime.

AUSSIE RULES

Only three recorded rugby matches have taken place at Meadow Lane. On 6 December 1912 England took on Australia and beat the tourists 5–3 in a closely fought Test match. Then on 3 March 1945 a combined Notts, Lincs & Derbys side lost 10–9 to the RAF and in 1986 Mansfield Marksmen played Fulham in a Rugby League encounter watched by fewer than 1,000 spectators – with such enthusiasm, no wonder there have been no games since!

ROCK ON, GIB!

County once took on Fulham in the territory of Gibraltar – it happened in May 1975. Two matches were arranged against the Cottagers within the space of three days, attracting a healthy turnout of tourists and ex-pats. The first game ended 2–2, but County edged the second match 3–2.

Two years later, County returned there to take on St Mirren in back-to-back games with the Jubilee Cup up for grabs. On 25 May the teams fought out a 2–2 draw and the following day they contested what was in effect the second leg, with County winning 2–1 and securing the trophy thanks to a 4–3 aggregate. An open-top bus was arranged for the return to Nottingham – until the club realised nobody really cared. . . .

SOMETHING IN RESERVE

The Magpies have operated a reserve team since the 1870s and it has played in various Midland leagues over the years. There have been several titles won, too – they are:

Midland Alliance	1890/91
Notts League	1903/04 & 1907/08
Central Alliance	1914/15
Midland League	1954/55
Midland Midweek League	1957/58
North Midland League	1973/74

WHAT? NO MORIARTY?

Put Paul Sherlock (1993–5), Richard Holmes (1998–2003) and Charlie Watson (1967–8) together in a County side and you could legitimately have a Sherlock Holmes and (Dr) Watson mystery to solve.

VERY SUPERSTITIOUS?

After remaining unbeaten for his first twelve games as boss at Meadow Lane, Steve Cotterill became overly superstitious as his team approached the finishing line during the 2009/10 season. The then Magpies boss revealed he had wore the same pair of pants and socks to every game, used the same pen to plan his tactics and wore the same black-and-white striped tie to each match. He also kept his coat on in the scorching sun as County beat Northampton Town 1–0.

'It was ridiculous really, I know,' he said. 'I kept saying to myself "what are you doing?" It's not like we would play any differently if I changed my tie! I was boiling at Northampton. I really wanted to take my coat off but I couldn't. It's silly I know, but that's the way I am.'

(UN) FRIENDLY FIRE

County took on Forest in a pre-season friendly in July 2007, but the game was marred by fighting on the pitch between both sets of supporters. Hundreds of fans ran on to the playing area and then County Chairman Jeff Moore said: 'It's an absolute disgrace. I just don't know what we do to prevent such idiocy that exists in our society today.'

Forest chief executive Mark Arthur added: 'Any people . . . causing serious havoc will receive banning orders from both the City Ground and matches we play away from home. We do not want any behaviour like that to tarnish the good name of Nottingham Forest.'

The fighting spilled out into the streets around Meadow Lane in one of the most violent meetings between the two old foes in modern times. Forest won the game 2–1.

FIXED PENALTY NOTICE

County have had some fine spot-kick takers over the years, but the very first player to score a penalty for the club was Jimmy Logan who fired home against Burton Wanderers during an FA Cup tie in 1894. Later that year, Elijah Allsopp (no relation to Danny – at least not that we know of) became the scorer of a penalty in league football when he struck home against Bury – one of two goals he scored during a 2–1 win.

The first penalty shoot-out was against neighbours Mansfield Town in 1975 during a County Cup semi-final. With the game ending 0–0, the shoot-out commenced and County triumphed 5–4. Three players have managed seven penalties in a single season – they are Arthur Green (1903/04), Kevin Randall (1972/73) and Ray O'Brien (1979/80).

On 22 September 1973, three County players managed to miss the same penalty! Kevin Randall took the first effort and missed and the referee demanded a retake because of encroachment. Don Masson suffered a similar fate, but again the official wasn't happy and ordered a third attempt. Brian Stubbs was the third and final taker and must have thought the law of averages would be on his side – wrong! He missed too! Fortunately, County still left Fratton Park with all three points having won 2–1.

CURTAIN-RAISERS

Since league football began in 1889/90, there have been 109 opening-day matches with 11 seasons lost to both world wars. Though County have endured three rotten starts where they have ended up on the end of a 5–0 drubbing away from home, the 'Pies best ever start was their most recent, with a 5–0 win over Bradford City in 2009/10 getting the boys off to a flyer that eventually saw the League Two title secured later in the campaign. No first game has quite exceeded the eight-goal thriller in 1987/88 when County and West Ham drew 4–4 at Meadow Lane – the highest aggregate opening day game in the club's history. Interestingly, the Magpies have begun the season away from home on 61 occasions compared with 49 home starts. The biggest opening-day away win was the 4–1 triumph at Crystal Palace in 1973.

The record in full, which doesn't give away many clues to the nature of County's coming season, is:

P: 110   W: 40   D: 29   L: 41   F: 136   A: 159

BOXING CLEVER?

The first Boxing Day fixtures were introduced in 1900 and County began their post-Christmas matches with a satisfying 1–0 win over Nottingham Forest. The Magpies have twice recorded 5–1 wins on Boxing Day – Middlesbrough (1914) and Swansea (1947) – with the heaviest defeat being a 4–0 thrashing by Manchester City. Though County have failed to win 49 of their 77 games on 26 December, when they do win, they have done it in style on more than occasion. Here is the complete record:

P: 78   W: 29   D: 15   L: 34   F: 100   A: 103

HAPPY NEW YEAR – OR NOT?

Although New Year's Day games seem to have been around for an eternity, only 34 matches have begun on 1 January in Notts County's league history. The first game in 1895 was a 2–1 defeat away to Bury, and this set the tone for the first six New Year's Day matches, all of which ended in defeat. In fact, County fans grew to dread the fixture with just two wins out of the first sixteen games and a dozen losses! Thankfully, things improved thereafter and the 'Pies have lost just six of their last eighteen New Year show-downs. Here is the complete record:

P: 34   W: 9   D: 7   L: 18   F: 43   A: 58

SEASON FINALES

Compared with 110 opening season games and 295 goals, when County finish a season off, they invariably do it with a goal flurry, historically speaking. Some 50 goals more have been scored in last-day games – and there have been some memorable final days of the league programme with the first ever, a 5–3 loss at home to Derby County, setting the tone, though none can top the 7–1 victory at Blackburn Rovers in 1891 when the 'Pies finished third in the fledgling Football League. Bizarrely, County lost the FA Cup final against Blackburn a week later by a more conservative score of 1–0! Eight years after that, already Division One champions Aston Villa handed out a 6–1 thrashing, avenging their 1–0 defeat suffered earlier in the campaign.

In 1925/26, relegated County beat champions Huddersfield Town 4–2 at Meadow Lane to leave the home fans scratching their heads as to why their team hadn't shown that kind of form on a regular basis. In fact, the Magpies beat all of the top six sides at home that season, scoring nineteen goals and conceding just four in the process. Other memorable games to send the Notts fans into the summer break with a smile include the 4–2 win over Nottingham Forest in 1957 – Forest were already promoted thanks to County's 2–0 win over promotion rivals Blackburn Rovers just eight days earlier, but at least the players restored faith by sending the Reds on their way with a good tonking. One game which gave County fans immense pleasure was – despite already having been relegated – when the 'Pies beat jinx team Luton Town 2–1 in May 1992 to ensure the Hatters joined them in the second tier – a suitable payback for all the misery the Bedfordshire side had caused County over the years with their unfathomable hex. Curiously, that was the only time the Magpies were demoted from Division One yet began the following season in Division One – unfortunately this was because the divisions were renamed following the inception of the Premier League – County still went down a league.

The complete record of last-day dramas is:

P: 110   W: 40   D: 23   L: 47   F: 169   A: 179

THANKS, DAVE

In April 1977 more than 10,500 people turned up for Dave Needham's testimonial at Meadow Lane. The cult hero centre-half won many friends during his time with the Magpies during which he racked up 469 appearances from 1965 to 1976. A Nottingham XI took on – and beat – a Midlands International XI 2–1 to send the big fella off in style.

THE GIANT-KILLING DECADE

Historically the Magpies have struggled against non-league sides in the FA Cup, but there was a decade that began in the mid-1950s when things went from bad to worse. It started in the first round in 1956/57 when Welsh minnows Rhyl left Meadow Lane having embarrassed a side three leagues above them with a 3–1 win. Then, in December 1959, Bath City left a crowd of almost 26,000 stunned following a 1–0 victory in Nottingham. Margate held County to a 1–1 draw in November 1961 too, and in December 1967 Runcorn triumphed 1–0 at Canal Street as the nightmarish run continued, though that was the last of the non-league head-shakers . . . at least for a while.

DO MENTION
THE WAR

The Magpies took on Dinamo Minsk on the 30th anniversary of Victory in Europe Day in May 1975. During an entertaining afternoon at Meadow Lane, eight goals were shared in a 4–4 draw, though Minsk won the penalty shoot-out by 4–3.

CROSSBAR CHALLENGE

Soccer AM paid a visit to the Notts County training ground during the 2008/09 season to give the County players a chance at the popular 'Crossbar Challenge' slot featured on the show. Sadly, none of the lads managed to strike the bar with the ball from the centre-spot, though there were a few near-misses.

WHAT A MANN

Arthur Mann was once Manchester City's record signing, but his chronic fear of flying eventually cost him his place in the side. In 1972 Mann arrived at Meadow Lane and embarked on a lengthy spell with the 'Pies – at least he didn't have to worry about flying off to take part in European games anymore! After playing 292 times over a seven-year period, Mann finally moved on leaving many friends behind in Nottingham. Tragically, Arthur was killed in an industrial accident in February 1999.

LET THERE BE LIGHT

Margate arrived at Meadow Lane in 1961 to contest their second round FA Cup replay having held County 1–1 on their own ground. The floodlights were normally only put at half-power during the pre-match warm up at most stadiums around England, but due to County's dilapidated, ageing lighting system, Margate believed the lighting would be turned to full during the match – sadly, it had been on full all the time! It just wasn't very good, but at least the 'Pies won 3–1 following an illuminating display.

STING RAY

Ray O'Brien achieved a rare feat in 1979/80 when he ended the campaign as the leading scorer with 10 goals from 41 league games – not bad for a full-back! Former Manchester United junior O'Brien slotted home seven penalties during the campaign and he twice converted two spot-kicks in one game. In all, O'Brien tucked away 19 penalties during his time at Meadow Lane and remains one of the club's most reliable spot-kick takers.

LAMBS TO THE SLAUGHTER

Prior to County becoming known as the Magpies in about 1890, the club was known as 'the Lambs'. The origins of the name are somewhat sketchy and can only really be guessed at – there used to be a gang of thugs in the Narrow Marsh area of the city who were also known as the Lambs and the same group were believed to be responsible for a pitch invasion when England played

Nottingham in 1817. The early County teams also had a reputation for rough-house tactics and the nickname could have been an association with the way the gangs of the day behaved, but surely in no more than an ironic way, i.e. NOT gentle as lambs? Mint sauce, anyone?

THE GHOSTS OF CHRISTMAS PAST

Unthinkable today that players would be made to play football on Christmas Day, isn't it? Sure, there are training sessions occasionally on Christmas morning at many clubs, but up until 1957, the Christmas Day fixture was a regular date on the football calendar.

The Magpies, for a while, revelled playing on 25 December and began in 1894 with a 5–0 win over Walsall. Though occasionally certain years were spared, the 'Pies then won their next seven Christmas Day fixtures up until 1911 when Manchester City spoiled their perfect record with a 1–0 win at Meadow Lane. Just as they'd won their opening eight Christmas games, County then failed to win their next eight, four of which were during the Midland League which operated in the First World War.

County have played Forest six times on Christmas Day, winning three, losing twice and drawing the other. The festive match continued up until 1957 when Barnsley won 3–2 at Meadow Lane and since that date, sense has prevailed and the 25 December match is a thing of the past.

Season	League	Opposition	Venue	Score
1894/95	Div 2	Walsall	H	5–0
1895/96	Div 2	Loughborough	H	2–0
1897/98	Div 1	Derby County	A	2–1

Season	League	Opposition	Venue	Score
1903/04	Div 1	Nottingham Forest	A	1–0
1905/06	Div 1	Nottingham Forest	A	2–1
1907/08	Div 1	Everton	H	2–1
1908/09	Div 1	Everton	A	1–0
1909/10	Div 1	Chelsea	H	2–1
1911/12	Div 1	Manchester City	H	0–1
1912/13	Div 1	Woolwich Arsenal	A	0–0
1913/14	Div 2	Nottingham Forest	H	2–2
1914/15	Div 1	Middlesbrough	A	0–1
1915/16	War	Leicester Fosse	H	1–2
1916/17	War	Hull City	A	0–2
1917/18	War	Nottingham Forest	H	0–1
1918/19	War	Nottingham Forest	A	0–2
1919/20	Div 1	Blackburn Rovers	H	5–0
1920/21	Div 2	Sheffield Weds	A	1–1
1922/23	Div 2	Fulham	H	1–0
1924/25	Div 1	Liverpool	H	1–2
1925/26	Div 1	Arsenal	A	0–3
1926/27	Div 2	Southampton	H	0–1
1928/29	Div 2	Southampton	H	1–1
1929/30	Div 2	Swansea City	A	2–3
1930/31	Div 3S	QPR	A	1–4
1931/32	Div 2	Port Vale	H	3–2
1933/34	Div 2	Millwall	H	0–1
1934/35	Div 2	Man United	A	1–2
1935/36	Div3S	Luton Town	H	0–3
1936/37	Div3S	Luton Town	A	1–2
1940/41	War	Nottingham Forest	A	4–2
1942/43	War	Lincoln City	A	1–8
1943/44	War	Lincoln City	H	2–5
1945/46	Div3S	Watford	A	2–7
1946/47	Div3S	Swindon Town	H	0–0
1948/49	Div3S	Northampton Town	A	2–1

Season	League	Opposition	Venue	Score
1950/51	Div 2	Chesterfield	A	0–0
1951/52	Div 2	Sheffield United	H	3–1
1952/53	Div 2	West Ham United	A	2–2
1953/54	Div 2	Birmingham City	A	0–3
1954/55	Div 2	Bristol Rovers	H	2–0
1957/58	Div 2	Barnsley	H	2–3

Total record:

P (league): 35	W: 14	D: 7	L: 14	F: 50	A: 50
P (wartime): 7	W: 1	D: 0	L: 6	F: 8	A:22

THE ITALIAN JOB

County flew off to Italy for an end of season tour in June 1971 and won both their matches. The Magpies beat Serie B side Rimini 4–2 and then beat Cesena 2–1 before returning home afterwards for a well-earned summer break.

TAKE A BOW, SON

He may have been coming to the end of an illustrious career, but Andy Gray spent a month in the colours of Notts County during the season of 1987/88 on loan from First Division side Aston Villa. With Garry Birtles also on board for the first time following his move from Nottingham Forest, the Magpies had a very attack-minded side as they kicked off the new campaign – and it showed. Gray played in the opening day 4–4 draw with Wigan Athletic and the 5–3 win at York, though curiously, he scored in neither game. With two 0–0 draws following in the league and a 0–0 draw with

Wolves in the League Cup, Gray's only goal in black and white stripes was in the replay at Molinuex – his former stomping ground – where County still went down 2–1. His month-long stint over, Gray returned to Villa Park having scored just once in six games and within a few years he'd become an anchorman on Sky Sports.

SUNDAY LEAGUE

Up until 1974, Sunday remained a church and family day in English football – sacrosanct in fact. But strikes across the country meant black-outs and power shortages, so on 20 January the Football League sanctioned matches on Sunday for the first time. Interestingly, the gate at Meadow Lane was several thousand higher than the average, with the home clash against Crystal Palace attracting just fewer than 15,000. A 3–1 defeat to Palace soured the landmark occasion, but with the power problems continuing for several months, the return Nottingham derby at the City Ground proved to be the second Sunday game of the season. The game, watched by 29,962, ended 0–0.

WE'VE STARTED, SO WE'LL FINISH

The 1946/47 season, severely affected by a merciless winter, saw many clubs having to stretch their normal season by two or three weeks in order to get all the rearranged games played. County were no different, wrapping up their campaign on 29 May 1947. Meadow Lane had suffered brutal frosts and was under several feet of snow on a couple of occasions as the winter bit hard and the end result was three games in five days to complete the Division Three (South) programme. On

24 May, County lost 2–0 to Southend United and two days later Leyton Orient also headed back south with maximum points following a narrow 1–0 win. Three days after, the 'Pies ended the season on a high, of sorts, with a 1–0 win over Reading guaranteeing them twelfth place in the table. Crack open the champagne!

THE 100% SEASON

Notts County have only once won all their games in one season – well, sort of. The 1939/40 campaign was just two games old when war was declared on Germany and league football was suspended indefinitely. After beating Bournemouth 2–1 at Meadow Lane and thrashing Cardiff City 4–2 at Ninian Park, the Magpies entered various regional leagues that featured numerous players, many no more than guests. When the war ended and league football resumed, County beat Bournemouth 1–0 at home before losing to Cardiff away. If you take in the 0–0 draw with Bristol City at the end of the 1938/39 season, the 'Pies were technically unbeaten from 6 May 1939 to 7 September 1946 – seven years and four months in total – now that's what you call an unbeaten run!

SONGS

You've heard them chanted on matchdays, some just once or twice, others every week – here is a selection of songs, without a 'Come on you 'Pies!' in sight:

I've never felt more like singing the blues,
when County win and Forest lose,
oh County, you got me singing the blues.

There's only one Jimmy Sirrel,
One Jimmy Sirrel, he's walking along singing his song,
walking in a Sirrel wonderland.

E-I-E-I-O
Up the Football League we go,
when we get promotion this is what we'll sing:
We are County, we are County, Hans Backe is our king.

(To the tune of 'Tragedy')
Notts County!
When the money's gone and we can't win one,
Notts County!
When the plumber lies and we don't know why,
It's hard to bear,
with no transfers pending, we're goin' nowhere . . .

County til I die,
I'm County 'til I die,
I'm Black and White,
'Cos it feels right,
I'm County 'til I die!

HARDLY PROLIFIC

There was an old joke in the early 1990s that suggested when negotiator Terry Waite was taken as a hostage and held for several years, the first thing he asked when his plane landed in the UK was, 'Has Garry Birtles scored yet?' The former Forest striker had transferred for big money to Manchester United, but endured a miserable time at Old Trafford, scoring just 11 in 58 appearances before returning to the City Ground. In 1987 he moved across the Trent for a season and a half but fared worse than he done in Manchester, scoring just 12 times in 88 appearances for the 'Pies. Forest till he dies?

LIKE FATHER, LIKE SON

There have only been two occasions where a father and son have both represented County. George Toone's playing career lasted from 1889 until 1902 and his son, George Jnr, also played for the club, though only once during the 1913/14 campaign. Harry Daft was with Notts from 1884 until 1895 and he followed in the footsteps of his father, Richard, who captained the club in the 1860s.

SEQUENCES

Longest unbeaten run: 21
In 1930, the Magpies drew their final home game of the season with Oldham Athletic and didn't taste defeat again until December when Southend United beat County 2–1 at Roots Hall – a run lasting the best part of seven months.

Most league home wins on the bounce: 14
County's fantastic winning-streak at Meadow Lane began with a 4–0 win over Gateshead in September 1959 and continued until Doncaster Rovers left with the points after a 4–3 victory the following March. The run formed the base of the club's promotion to Division Three after finishing runners-up to Walsall.

Most home games unbeaten: 26
From April 1970 until August 1971, Jimmy Sirrel's County went 27 league and cup games undefeated at Meadow Lane. The run included 22 wins and 4 draws and 66 goals scored and just 12 conceded – less than one every two games.

Most away games unbeaten: 10
County ended the 1970/71 season unbeaten in their final two away games and then failed to lose the first eight games of the 1971/72 campaign – a run of 6 wins and 4 draws.

Consecutive clean sheets: 7
County failed to concede a goal in seven successive games during the 1970/71 season before Peterborough earned a 1–1 draw at London Road. The 'Pies also went six games without letting a goal in during the 2009/10 campaign.

Consecutive games scored: 39
County have a proud record of 39 matches on the bounce when they managed to find the net at least once – and that's something the club has achieved on two occasions. The sequence began on the final day of the 1929/30 season and ended 11 months later with a 0–0 draw at Northampton Town.

Successive league defeats: 7
Unfortunately County have suffered seven successive reverses on three separate occasions. The most recent seven losses in a row came during the 1983/84 campaign when only Brian 'Killer' Kilcline's goal at Norwich earned a 1–1 draw and stopped the rot, though County were still relegated at the end of that season.

Most games without a win: 20
County endured a horrific set of results in 1996/97 during one of the club's worst seasons on record. The run cost manager Colin Murphy his job and ended in relegation.

Most home games without a win: 14
The Magpies failed to win any of their last fourteen matches at Meadow Lane during the 1979/80 season, drawing eight and losing six from 24 November 1979 until August 1980 when Bolton Wanderers were dispatched 2–1. That was the start of an unbeaten home run of ten games – from one extreme to the other – such is the life of a County fan, eh?

Most away league games without a win: 29
County failed to win any of their last twenty away matches of the 1992/93 campaign and also didn't win any of their first nine trips on the road the following season. Somewhat ironically, the run ended at champions-elect Crystal Palace's Selhurst Park with an unexpected 2–1 win.

HARRY'S GAME

Forget Ian Rush, Denis Law or Alan Shearer when you're in the pub next time and the trivia questions are flying around – just ask: 'who is the record FA Cup goalscorer of all-time?' As a County fan, you will be able to inform them that Harry Cursham holds the record with 49 strikes in the competition and that was from just 36 appearances. Rush managed a measly 44 during his career and Law a paltry 41, but Cursham remains comfortably the best. In fact, it would have been 51 had his two goals in another cup tie not later been declared void. Cursham bagged four hat-tricks, scored four on one occasion and managed one double hat-trick along the way to creating a little bit of history. Fittingly, he also scored the Magpies' first FA Cup goal in November 1877 during a 1–1 draw with Sheffield at Trent Bridge.

HIGH FIVES

County's 13–0 FA Cup win over Basford Rovers in 1886 features two scorers who both managed five goals. Harry Daft and F.E. Burton both fell one short of a double hat-trick in the game and County's run to the sixth round averaged five goals per game, scoring thirty in just six ties. The feat was achieved again when Bertie Mills netted five times during a 9–0 victory over Barnsley in 1927.

JIMMY SAID IT . . .

Legendary County manager Jimmy Sirrel was renowned for his pearls of wisdom. Here are a few of his best lines.

'The best team always wins. The rest is only gossip.'

'I couldn't just give you one player who I think was my best signing. If you go through them, you'll find lots of players: Raddy Avramovic, Iain McCulloch and little John Chiedozie . . . they could all play.'

'Brian Clough and I were very friendly. He was a nice person, but a bit bombastic about his football. He seemed to be able to handle players successfully and was a tremendously successful manager for his time. Indeed, I was at his funeral.'

'Ask any kid what he knows about Notts County, and he'll tell you they're the oldest football team in the world. By the time I've finished, he'll know a lot more.'

'In my opinion the goalkeeper is the number one man in your team. You start with a point, and if he doesn't lose a goal, you get that. So if you score one, you've won.'

MAD HATTERS

Luton Town are one of the Magpies' main bogey teams. The basis of being a jinx side is that there is no particular reason to explain a miserable set of results over the years and Luton fit firmly into this category. Of the 32 league meetings in Nottingham, County have won just eight and away from home, it gets worse – County have won just four of their 32 visits to Kenilworth Road making for an awful record overall during which the Hatters have avoided defeat in 52 meetings out of 64 – here are the stats:

P	W	D	L	F	A
64	12	19	33	67	120

CAN WE PLAY YOU EVERY WEEK?

One team 'Pies fans would love to play regularly is Northampton Town, such is County's dominance in the fixture – especially at home. With 18 wins out of

24 in Nottingham and just 10 defeats out of 24 visits to Northampton, the total record makes very pleasant reading:

P	W	D	L	F	A
48	25	10	13	75	60

HOMERS

County's battles with Wrexham over the years have been successful at home, but poor away. For some reason, each team dominates the home fixture with away victories something of a rarity. Notts County have won 14 and drawn 8 of the 24 matches played at home, while in contrast, Wrexham have lost just 4 of the 24 clashes at the Racecourse Ground. With this in mind, it seems a fairly logical bet for a home win on the fixed odds coupons when these two teams meet next!

100% RECORD

One team which dreads travelling to Nottingham is Scunthorpe United – a team which has managed to lose every time it has played at Meadow Lane. There have been eight visits in the league and cup by the Iron over a 41-year period and they've lost the lot! In fact, they've only managed to score on two occasions.

GROUNDS FOR CONCERN

Formed in 1862, it's perhaps no surprise that to learn that the Magpies have had many different homes over the years. With the first 40 years or so seeing numerous venues, it's amazing the club didn't change their name to Nottingham Nomads or Notts Wanderers. Without further ado, here is a complete list of places that County have called home over the past 148 years.

Park Hollow/Meadows Cricket Ground

The Magpies' first home was Park Hollow – a private park next to Nottingham Castle where the fledgling club initially played matches among members. It wasn't until December 1864 that Notts played a match – 20-a-side at that – on the nearby Meadows Cricket Ground. This would become home until 1877, though for special occasions Trent Bridge Cricket Ground would be hired.

Beeston/Castle Cricket Ground

County moved in October 1877 to Beeston and occasionally used another cricket ground closer to the town centre, such as it was back in those days. Trent Bridge was used for the odd game and on 30 November 1878, the 'Pies took on Derbyshire in one of the world's first floodlit matches, though the lights were nothing but lanterns suspended on tall poles. Exactly two years later the club moved to the Castle Cricket Ground, where they played until 1883. Previously, Nottingham Forest had been renting Trent Bridge from its new owners, Nottinghamshire County Cricket Club, but they left in 1883 for their new ground in Lenton.

Trent Bridge

Hard to imagine Nottinghamshire CCC or their ground staff sanctioning football matches on the hallowed Trent Bridge turf, isn't it? Things were a little different at that time, however, with the cricketers not having a favoured strip – more a suitable patch of the ground was selected and there they played! County's first game as permanent tenants of Trent Bridge was against Walsall Swifts in September 1883 and two years later the club finally turned professional. In doing so, they became founder members of the Football League in 1888. A decade later, a half-time and results scoreboard was built and this first came into use on 3 December 1898 for a match against Everton. Who said County weren't trendsetters?

Other Venues

Naturally, cricket still took priority at Trent Bridge and each September and April, County had to find alternative places to play their home games. The Meadows and the Castle Cricket Ground were utilised again and County also used whatever ground Forest happened to be calling home at the time. County's final match at Trent Bridge was on 16 April 1910 against Aston Villa.

A Home of Our Own

In 1910, the 'Pies finally moved to Meadow Lane which was, at that time, a piece of open ground next to a cattle market. When the patch of land had been secured, a Main Stand was erected in just nine days at a cost of £3,000 and when complete with furnishings and fittings, the total cost was a not-insubstantial £10,000. Meadow Lane was opened with a glamour derby game against Forest on 3 September 1910. The match, watched by a crowd of approximately 28,000, was drawn 1–1 with Billy Matthews, formerly of Aston Villa, scoring the first County ever goal at the club's new home. The Magpies were up and running and, more than 100 years later, Meadow Lane is still a very happy home for the club.

I'VE STARTED … BUT I WON'T FINISH

A total of 11 matches featuring County have failed to reach a natural conclusion over the years, having been abandoned by the official for one reason or another.

The first to be called to a halt in November 1889 was curious in that the 2–2 draw with Stoke actually lasted 90 minutes, but the game was declared null and void because it had been played in thick fog! The replayed match also ended in a draw, this time 1–1. Fog was again the culprit in 1901 when the match at Bolton Wanderers was called off after 25 minutes with the score at 0–0 – County won the rearranged game 1–0.

Two years later, in 1903, County were trailing 1–0 when heavy rain forced the abandonment of the match at Aston Villa – the weather couldn't rescue the 'Pies in the rearranged game, however, with Villa running out winners 2–1.

Rain saved the day again with County 2–0 down at Bolton in 1906, though when the game was replayed not long after, Bolton will have felt justification in winning by exactly the same scoreline.

At White Hart Lane in 1912, just 8 minutes were remaining when the referee decided the fog was too thick to continue. The trouble was County were 3–1 up against hosts Spurs, so the locals weren't too upset, though three weeks later the Magpies completed the game and justice was seen to be done as County triumphed 3–0.

In 1934 rain halted the still scoreless league game with Bradford Park Avenue at Meadow Lane with just 16 minutes on the clock – County won the re-run 1–0. Three years later, on Christmas Day 1937, fog was the cause once more with the 'Pies trailing 1–0 at Gillingham, though the Gills triumphed in the rearranged game 2–1.

The four remaining abandonments were all at home: Halifax (rain) 1960, Millwall (rain) 1965, Tranmere (fog) 1965 and finally Burnley (a touch of frost, minus David Jason) 1976. All these teams were either drawing with or beating the 'Pies at the time, so there were few complaints from the home fans.

The rearranged games saw a 1–1 draw with Halifax, a 2–1 loss to Millwall and a 2–1 loss to Tranmere. Thankfully the last game saw County beat Burnley 5–1.

The total record for how the abandoned games stood is:
Winning: 1 Drawing: 5 Losing: 5   For: 6 Against: 11

The record for the rearranged fixtures is:
Won: 4   Drawn: 2   Lost: 5   For: 16   Against: 13

JUST THE TICKET

St Kitts-born former County defender Tristan Benjamin made more than 300 appearances for the club in the 1970s. A popular figure at Meadow Lane, Benjamin was a bus driver for Nottingham City Transport and is now understood to be a teacher of trainee bus drivers.

TOMMY LAWTON SAID IT ...

One of the club's all-time greats, Tommy Lawton also produced some of the best quotes.

'They say where there's no sense, there's no feeling. That's probably why I scored so many with my head.'
Tommy was deadly in the air

'I can't forget the day I joined Notts County – it was 18 November 1947. At the time I was playing for Chelsea and Arthur Stollery was the manager of Notts. He had been the masseuse at Stamford Bridge and we had been very good friends there. Suddenly Arthur left after a disagreement with the chairman and Arthur asked me before leaving that if he got fixed up somewhere else would I be prepared to join him? I said yes, but thought nothing more about it till I got a call out of the blue from him at Meadow Lane.'

Tommy on his sensational move from aristocrats Chelsea to third-tier County

'I spent four-and-a-half memorable years at Notts County. Believe me, there were far too happy memories to pick out one above another.'

Tommy, who many believe sacrificed his England career by moving out of the top flight

'I made Nottingham my adopted city. That says enough about my feelings for the place. We broke all records both home and away with support at the time. Numerous First Division clubs were interested but I had no hesitation in signing.'

The legend that is Lawton

'My time at Notts as a manager lasted just eleven months – for both the club and myself it was a complete disaster. It's a time of my life best forgotten.'

Swapping playing for life behind a desk never suited the great man

WHERE'S THE CELEB 'PIES?

Only two County fans are well known to the rest of the country and neither are likely to win many popularity contests. The first is one of Britain's most notorious serial killers of all time, Dr Harold Shipman, who was apparently a Magpies fan, and Kenneth Clarke MP is the other – no cool rock bands or actors, then? Maybe we'll just have to make a few up!

NASTY RASH

Algerian midfielder Rachid Harkouk was nicknamed 'Rash the Smash' because of his penchant for long-range shooting. The Chelsea-born County star played 174 times for the 'Pies between 1980 and 1985, scoring 52 goals in the process. He represented Algeria at the 1986 World Cup, though he had moved to pastures new by that time.

ROCK ON, TOMMY

Tommy Lawton died on 6 November 1996 – here is a selection of tributes for the club legend:

David McVay (writer, author and former County player)
'The one thing Tommy Lawton earned was respect and that's a commodity money can't buy in these days of multi-million transfer fees and wages. He never ducked an issue or flinched a controversial challenge.

He was prepared to call a spade a spade and say what he thought about the high and mighty and the humble. Tommy Lawton remains a giant in the beautiful game . . .

his death means another vital link with the game and a way of life has gone forever.'

Jackie Sewell
'Tom was the best centre forward I ever saw, no problem. Not only was he the best there'd been in the air, he had two exceptionally good feet. The man had incredible presence and brought a tremendous amount of pleasure to spectators. I couldn't speak highly enough about the man. I'm very, very sad.'

Wilf Mannion
'Tommy was truly a great player, one of the best centre forwards there has been anywhere. As a bloke he fitted into the set-up like anyone else. There was always a good camaraderie and atmosphere among the players. In those days we played for the love of the game.'

Denis Compton
'I had all the time in the world for Tommy, both as a player and a person . . . Tommy was a great, great centre forward – the best I've seen or played with.'

Tom Finney
'I played with some terrific centre forwards, but Tommy was the best . . . Tommy was a Lancashire lad like me, with a lovely sense of humour. He helped in the dressing-room camaraderie as much as anybody did.'

And finally, David McVay again
'I fancy the memory of Tommy Lawton and his days of soccer innocence will remain. We'll be looking for you at the far post, Tommy.'

CLUB LEGEND:
DEAN YATES (1985–95)

Appearances: 394
Goals: 7
Date of Birth: 26 October 1967
Birthplace: Leicester

Dean Yates broke into a County side already heading for relegation in April 1985. He made his debut during a 3–2 defeat at home to Wimbledon, though Yates would prove to be one of the few highlights of a disappointing campaign.

County were far from impressive the following season, just about mustering an 8th-place finish, but the teenage Yates had at least made the number 6 shirt his own playing in 57 of County's 59 games in all competitions – more than any other player.

For the next 5 years, Yates became the rock of County's defence, rarely missing a game and popping up with the odd vital goal too, and was an integral member of Neil Warnock's side which won successive promotions back to Division One. It was Yates who scored the club's first goal back in the top flight as he headed home the winner in a 1–0 win over Southampton in August 1991. County were relegated at the end of that season and Yates would suffer a crippling knee injury that saw him miss the next two seasons, making his long-awaited return in the last game of the 1993/94 campaign.

GOAL! FACTS AND FIGURES

Les Bradd scored 137 goals in all competitions between 1967 and 1977 and is the club's record goal-scorer. Bradd joined from Rotherham and left for Stockport County after a decade of leading the Magpies' line with aplomb.

Tom Keetley holds the record for most league goals in one season having managed 39 during the 1930/31 campaign that saw the club win the Division Three (South) title in a canter. Two more in the FA Cup give him an even more impressive haul of 41 all told. With ten hat-tricks, Keetley also holds the record for most trebles for the club.

While on the subjects of hat-tricks, the quickest treble of all time was scored by Ian Scanlon in November 1974 when he managed three goals inside 2 minutes 45 seconds, though County still only managed a 3–3 draw against Sheffield Wednesday, despite Scanlon's best efforts.

The fastest goal on record for County is Barrie Jones's strike after just 6 seconds against Torquay in March 1962.

CROWD CONTROL

County's best average attendance is 35,176, set during the Division Three South championship season of 1949/50 when Tommy Lawton fever was at its height and the Magpies won the title. The lowest is 4,258, posted during the disastrous 1996/97 campaign.

The biggest recorded crowd the club has played in front of is 61,003 at Liverpool in an FA Cup fourth round tie on 29 January 1949. County lost 1–0 and while that record has remained intact for 61 years, cup draws that include trips to Manchester United or Arsenal are the only way the record is likely to be broken any time soon.

PROPER CHARLIE

Charlie Palmer's winning goal against Nottingham Forest on 12 February 1994, watched by 17,911 Meadow Lane fans, resulted in the day being re-Christened 'Sir Charles Palmer Day' and, in some sections, the day is still celebrated by County fans. Palmer played for the club 221 times between 1988 and 1994, and describes the goal as 'the sweetest of my career' with his sweeping header sending the home fans crazy – despite playing in a kit that resembled a barcode!

SOL'S SOLITARY GAME

Capped by England 73 times and fresh from winning the 2009 FA Cup final, Sol Campbell became arguably the highest-profile signing Notts County FC have ever made, though some would argue Tommy Lawton's arrival was even more dramatic. That, however, is an argument for another day. The signing was supposed to have been the first of many stellar names attracted to Meadow Lane by former England manager Sven-Goran Eriksson, but when questions began to be raised about the club's owners, Munto Finance, Campbell began to get itchy feet. His one and only appearance was away to Morecambe in September 2009 – he walked out on the Magpies three days later and eventually agreed a contract termination, rejoining Arsenal during the January 2010 transfer window instead.

KEEP YOUR ENEMIES CLOSER …

With just 300 yards separating Meadow Lane from Forest's City Ground, the two Nottingham clubs are officially the two closest grounds in England. The title of closest grounds in Britain goes to Dundee and Dundee United.

KILLER MOVE!

Cult terrace hero Brian 'Killer' Kilcline moved just about as far away from football as he could when he retired. He started a life on the ocean waves – of sorts – by living on a barge in the Midlands and renovating houses in Yorkshire. Best of all, and in keeping with his maverick, edgy reputation as a player, he is also a professional arm wrestler – what else would you expect from Killer, surely a movie waiting to happen? We're not worthy!

FOOTBALL LEAGUE GROUP CUP

Sometimes you just have to hold your hands up and admit – that was a really bad idea. Case in point, the ill-fated Football League Group Cup of 1981/82. Held for just one season as a replacement for the Anglo-Scottish Cup, the crowds were poor and the overall interest was minimal at best. County played all their games in pre-season and began with a trip to Lincoln City, drawing 1–1 at Sincil Bank. Then it was off to London Road to take on Peterborough United where 2,483 fans witnessed another 1–1 draw. The third game in a week was also away and ended in a 3–0 loss at Norwich City, meaning the Magpies didn't progress, but then neither did the competition which failed to survive beyond its inaugural season.

Z IS FOR ...

The Zenith Data Systems Cup – formerly known as the Full Members' Cup, which ran from 1985 to 1992, but County only entered the competition in its final two years. The crowds weren't great but there was the dangling carrot of playing the final at Wembley Stadium. Despite beating Port Vale 1–0, the Magpies drew 2–2 with Sunderland at Meadow Lane and went out 3–1 on penalties. In 1991/92, County saw off both Sheffield clubs on their way to the semi-finals of the competition drawing 3–3 with Sheffield United before beating Sheffield Wednesday 1–0 at Meadow Lane. The chance for a place in the final meant a semi-final against Leicester City and 11,559 fans turned out to see the game, which unfortunately the Foxes triumphed 2–1 in after extra time.

THE LONG ...
AND THE SHORT OF IT

Standing at 5ft 3in, Steve Holder is believed to be the shortest player to ever represent Notts County. Holder made his debut in April 1970 against Northampton – his only appearance for the club. The tallest player was also a club legend – Albert Iremonger – who stood at 6ft 5in in County's goal.

FLICK THE SWITCH

Floodlights were in place and in use by 1953 and were first switched on for a friendly with Derby County on 23 March of that year. They were basic and short-term and in 1962 the club installed a new set of lights mounted on taller pylons and these were first put to use on 11 October 1962 for a match against Port Vale – a 1–0 win watched by 14,320 fans.

WOODSTOCK COUNTY

On 10 May 1969, things got groovy as Meadow Lane hosted Nottingham's 11-hour 1969 Pop and Blues festival presented by Radio One DJs John Peel and Ed Stewart. Among the acts on the day were Pink Floyd, Fleetwood Mac, The Move and Status Quo. Far out, man!

MOST WINS IN A ROW

The best run of successive victories is ten, achieved in 1997/98 by Sam Allardyce's County, with six of those wins coming away from Meadow Lane.

PLAYER OF THE YEAR

Voted for by supporters since its introduction in 1964/65, the Player of the Year award is the highest honour a player can have bestowed on him by the fans. Though Shaun Murphy, Mark Stallard and Phil Turner have won it twice, only club legend Don Masson has won it outright three times. Ian Richardson has also picked up the gong on three occasions, though in 1999 he shared the award with Darren Ward.

2009/10	Ben Davies	Midfielder
2008/09	Matt Halmshaw	Winger
2007/08	Kevin Pilkington	Goalkeeper
2006/07	Mike Edwards	Defender
2005/06	David Pipe	Defender
2004/05	Ian Richardson	Defender
2003/04	Ian Richardson	Defender
2002/03	Mark Stallard	Striker
2001/02	Danny Allsopp	Striker
2000/01	Mark Stallard	Striker
1999/2000	Alex Dyer	Striker
1998/99	Darren Ward & Ian Richardson	
1997/98	Gary Jones	Striker
1996/97	Matt Redmile	Defender
1995/96	Shaun Murphy	Defender
1994/95	Shaun Murphy	Defender
1993/94	Phil Turner	Midfielder
1992/93	Dave Smith	Midfielder
1991/92	Steve Cherry	Goalkeeper
1990/91	Craig Short	Defender
1989/90	Phil Turner	Midfielder
1988/89	Chris Withe	Defender
1987/88	Geoff Pike	Striker
1986/87	Dean Yates	Defender

1985/86	Tristan Benjamin	Defender
1984/85	Pedro Richards	Defender
1983/84	Trevor Christie & John Chiedozie	
1982/83	Raddy Avramovic	Goalkeeper
1981/82	Iain McCulloch	Striker
1980/81	Don Masson	Midfielder
1979/80	David Hunt	Midfielder
1978/79	Eric McManus	Goalkeeper
1977/78	Mick Vinter	Midfielder
1976/77	Arthur Mann	Striker
1975/76	Ray O'Brien	Defender
1974/75	Joe Brindley	Defender
1973/74	Don Masson	Midfielder
1972/73	Roy Brown	Goalkeeper
1971/72	Les Bradd	Striker
1970/71	Brian Stubbs	Defender
1969/70	Dave Needham	Defender
1968/69	Don Masson	Midfielder
1967/68	Keith Smith	Defender
1966/67	Alex Gibson	Defender
1965/66	Brian Bates	Midfielder
1964/65	George Smith	Goalkeeper

GREAT SCOT – WE'VE SCORED!

Scottish side Queen's Park were the team to beat back in the late 1800s. Formed in 1867, they remained unbeaten for 9 years! In the eighth year of that run, Notts County travelled north of the border to take on the best team around as a gauge of how far the club had to go to be able to take on the big boys, but though they left with a 6–0 defeat, much was learned – in particular the theory it might not be wise to play them again! However, the teams did meet again just two months later and County managed to score during another loss – and in doing so became the first English club to ever manage to net against them. For the record, Queen's Park were eventually beaten by Wanderers in February 1876 and looking at the club today, it's been pretty much downhill ever since for the Scots.

PHIL TURNER SAID IT ...

Phil Turner skippered the Magpies four times at Wembley and is one of the club's all-time greats. The former crowd favourite never hid his enthusiasm when he played – or spoke about playing . . .

'I was so proud last week when I got the Player of the Year trophy, but emotion just took over at Wembley and I couldn't stop myself crying as I went up the steps. To receive that trophy and turning to face the fans was an absolutely marvellous moment and I couldn't have been any prouder.'

Magpies skipper Phil Turner after the play-off win against Tranmere

'We proved people wrong this season and we'll continue to do it. No one will give us a cat in hell's chance – but we'll show them. That will be the perfect stage for us. We always rise to the occasion and next year will be no different. We're looking forward to taking on Liverpool and Manchester United. It's going to be a tremendous summer, thinking about Anfield and Old Trafford. I can't wait for next season to start.'

Turner on the implications of victory in that 1991 play-off final against Tranmere

'Winning promotion was a real squad effort. It wasn't just down to the eleven who played and I felt sorry for those who didn't play. But the manager had got to upset some and it was great to see everyone respond.'

Turner – the consummate skipper

'It was a magnificent day and, from a personal point of view, it's been a long time coming since my time in the Fourth Division with Lincoln City. But ever since I've been involved with Notts, we've had nothing but success – and we deserve it.'

Turner reflects on his path from the bottom to the top tier

ANOTHER PROPER CHARLIE

County's first victory was in 1867 when Notts beat Sheffield 1–0 at Bramall Lane. Charles Rothera scored the goal of what, in the grand scheme of things, was a quite momentous day in the club's history.

THE DIRTY DOZEN (OR SO)

A crowd at the away match between County and Crewe Alexandra was described in one newspaper as 'a few dozen'! Hard to imagine a crowd lower than the average Sunday League game, but this wasn't a game that had the locals queueing up in advance! It's thought this is the lowest crowd County ever played in front of and, if taken literally, could be numbered as low as 24!

A WHEELY GOOD SONG

There are many different stories about where the 'Wheelbarrow Song' first started and maybe there's a bit truth in all of them. Some believe it was when a groundsman was on the pitch at half time with a wheelbarrow. As he cut the corner of the pitch near the corner flag, the wheel fell off and a terrace chant was born. Another version is that the song derived from an interview with former 'Pies boss Neil Warnock during which he said: 'When I first came to Notts County all I had was a wheelbarrow . . . and the wheel fell off that!' The most enduring and likely explanation, however, was that it began on 17 April 1990.

The 'Pies were playing Shrewsbury Town away and were 2–0 down with less than 10 minutes to go. The locals, happy with their lot, began singing some kind of odd colloquial song that the visiting fans took to be 'I had a wheelbarrow and the wheel fell off' (as you do). Bemused and amused, the County throng began singing the song back, obviously with their own interpretation. The effect was remarkable with the 'Pies scoring two late goals to pinch a 2–2 draw. The comeback was associated with the weird and wonderful song and a legend was born – just don't ask anyone what it means!

CLUB LEGEND: MARK DRAPER (1988–94)

Appearances: 277
Goals: 49
Born: 11 November 1970
Birthplace: Nottingham

Of all the players to come through County's youth system, Mark Draper is among the very best. The technically gifted midfielder made his debut during the 1988/89 season, forcing his way into the manager's plans with a series of displays that belied his tender years.

Like fellow youth team graduates Dean Yates and Tommy Johnson, Draper quickly became an indispensible member of the first team at Meadow Lane. His vision and passing ability quickly made him a target for bigger clubs, but he would remain a County player for a total of six seasons.

There was no doubt that he deserved a crack at playing for a top side with even better players around him, but for one reason and another, it never really happened for Draper who joined Leicester City in 1994 for £1.25m.

His highlight was probably the stunning goal he scored against Sunderland on the final day of the 1992/93 season – a win that prevented County going down for a second successive season. After just one season with Leicester, Draper moved to Aston Villa for almost triple the fee he cost the Foxes and stayed at Villa Park for five years, winning an England call-up in the process. After a loan spell in Spain with Rayo Vallecano he returned to England with Southampton, though his time on the south coast was dogged by injury.

In 2009, Draper returned to Meadow Lane as the club's kit man.

10 DAVID v GOLIATH FA CUP TIES

County have had a chequered past against non-league teams over the years – but have things improved or got worse? Here is the last decade of FA Cup ties against so-called minnows . . .

8 December 2000, First Round
Gravesend & Northfleet 1–2 Notts County
County faced Gravesend at Gillingham's Priestfield Stadium and Mark Stallard put the Magpies in front after just 3 minutes. Andy Hughes doubled the lead before Jimmy Jackson pulled one back but the visitors held on for a welcome victory.

16 November 2002, First Round
Southport 4–2 Notts County
With the *Match of the Day* cameras in town sniffing an upset, County travelled to Haig Avenue for a first round tie with Southport who were two divisions below their more illustrious visitors. Things seemed to be going according to plan when Danny Allsopp struck twice to give County a 2–0 lead, but Darren Caskey's sending-off proved to be a major blow for the Magpies. Steve Pickford pulled one back before half time and then equalised on the hour to send the home fans wild – but there was worse to come. Peter Thomson fired the hosts

in front and then Pickford raced through to seal his hat-trick and a earn a place in FA Cup folklore.

9 November 2003, First Round
Notts County 7–2 Shildon
One of the highest-scoring games Meadow Lane has seen in a long time was the Magpies' first round FA Cup tie back in 2003 when the home fans lapped up seven goals against Shildon who had become one of the lowest-ranked sides ever to reach that stage of the competition. Nick Fenton and Clive Platt (2) put County 3–0 up inside 20 minutes but Shildon rallied through goals from Middleston and Barnes to make it 3–2. However, further County goals from Kevin Nicholson, Ian Richardson, Tony Barras and Paul Heffernan ensured the north-east minnows went home dejected, though with their heads still held high following their epic adventure.

6 December 2003, Second Round
Gravesend & Northfleet 1–2 Notts County
The second meeting between the clubs in three years attracted the Sky Sports cameras but County were up for the battle in an exact repeat of the 2000 tie. On a bitterly cold evening, Steven Perkins fired the non-leaguers ahead on the stroke of half time to send the home fans wild, but the visitors fought back to equalise through Nick Fenton, and then Clive Platt struck deep into injury time to book the Magpies a third round tie at Middlesbrough and break Gravesend supporters' hearts.

13 November 2004, First Round
Notts County 2–0 Woking
No dramas or shocks as County put in a polished professional display against Conference side Woking at Meadow Lane. Julien Baudet's penalty put the Magpies

ahead in the first half and an injury-time goal from Gavin Gordon sealed the victory and set up a second round tie against Swindon Town.

10 November 2007, First Round
Notts County 3–0 Histon
Histon proved to be little more than an irritation as County cruised into the second round with a comfortable victory. All three goals came in the second half after a tepid first 45 minutes and were the work of Lawrie Dudfield (2) and Hector Sam, who sealed the win for a confident Magpies side.

1 December 2007, Second Round
Notts County 0–1 Havant & Waterlooville
Despite the visitors already having seen off York City, County were expected to ease past the Blue Square South side with comparative ease and take their place in the third round proper. However, it proved to be anything but a walk in the park as Havant inflicted one of County's most embarrassing defeats of all time. County were poor and simply couldn't break down a dogged Havant defence and the longer the game went on, the more edgy the home fans became – with good reason. Finally, the inevitable happened – a long ball forward saw Keystone Cops-style defending of the highest order to allow Tony Taggart to seal a famous win for the Hawks. Havant would go on to beat Swansea City and twice take the lead at Anfield against Liverpool before finally bowing out against the former Champions League winners.

8 November 2008, First Round
Sutton United 0–1 Notts County
County made hard work of their first round tie with Sutton United – a team placed some three divisions below

the Magpies. Sutton, who once knocked out a top-flight Coventry City, were dogged but rarely threatened during a dull game on a pitch that resembled a cabbage patch, and the game was settled when Richard Butcher headed home on 75 minutes.

30 November 2008, Second Round
Notts County 1–1 Kettering Town
County found non-league Kettering a tough nut to crack at Meadow Lane. With the game played on a Sunday and the draw for the next round already made, the winners would face Eastwood Town in the next round and a likely passage into the lucrative third round draw. The visitors started the brighter and went ahead when Brett Solkhon opened the scoring to send the travelling fans wild. Kettering should have been 3–0 by the break, but missed two clear-cut chances. The Pies scrambled back into the game when Sean Canham poked home from close range towards the end of the first half – there was no further scoring and the match went to a replay.

10 December 2008, Second Round Replay
Kettering Town 2–1 Notts County
Despite being outplayed for long periods of the first meeting between the two teams, County looked up for the battle in the Rockingham Road replay and went ahead when Jay Smith scored a peach of a goal from the edge of the box. However, two second-half goals in two minutes proved enough to put the hosts through. Brett Solkhon headed home to make it 1–1 before Gareth Seddon fired home the winner which resigned County to their only defeat to non-league opposition – so far – in the twenty-first century.

ONE FOR SORROW?

County are one of the few clubs in England who can legitimately claim to hold something of an Indian Sign over Manchester United – well, a decent record if nothing else! The Reds have failed to beat the 'Pies on 29 occasions out of a total of 50, winning 21 in total.

County's complete record against Man United (home and away) is:

P: 50   W: 14   D: 15   L: 21   F: 64   A: 79

The results, with the most recent first, are as follows:

18/1/1992	Notts County	1–1	Man United
17/8/1991	Man United	2–0	Notts County
14/4/1984	Notts County	1–0	Man United
27/12/1983	Man United	3–3	Notts County
14/5/1983	Notts County	3–2	Man United
11/12/1982	Man United	4–0	Notts County
20/3/1982	Notts County	1–3	Man United
31/10/1981	Man United	2–1	Notts County
19/4/1975	Notts County	2–2	Man United
12/10/1974	Man United	1–0	Notts County
26/12/1934	Notts County	1–0	Man United
25/12/1934	Man United	2–1	Notts County
21/4/1934	Notts County	0–0	Man United
9/12/1933	Man United	1–2	Notts County
18/3/1933	Notts County	1–0	Man United
5/11/1932	Man United	2–0	Notts County
5/3/1932	Notts County	1–2	Man United
24/10/1931	Man United	3–3	Notts County
5/4/1926	Man United	0–1	Notts County
2/4/1926	Notts County	0–3	Man United
21/2/1923	ManUnited	1–1	Notts County

10/2/1923	Notts County	1–6	Man United
1/5/1920	Notts County	0–2	Man United
26/4/1920	Man United	0–0	Notts County
30/1/1915	Man United	2–2	Notts County
26/9/1914	Notts County	4–2	Man United
8/3/1913	Notts County	1–2	Man United
2/11/1912	Man United	2–1	Notts County
2/3/1912	Man United	2–0	Notts County
28/10/1911	Notts County	0–1	Man United
18/3/1911	Notts County	1–0	Man United
12/11/1910	Man United	0–0	Notts County
25/9/1909	Notts County	3–2	Man United
6/9/1909	Man United	2–1	Notts County
13/4/1909	Notts County	0–1	Man United
1/1/1909	Man United	4–3	Notts County
11/4/1908	Man United	0–1	Notts County
14/12/1907	Notts County	1–1	Man United
5/1/1907	Notts County	3–0	Man United
8/9/1906	Man United	0–0	Notts County
27/3/1897	Man United	1–1	Notts County
19/12/1896	Notts County	3–0	Man United
14/12/1895	Man United	3–0	Notts County
23/11/1895	Notts County	0–2	Man United
20/4/1895	Man United	3–3	Notts County
15/12/1894	Notts County	1–1	Man United
26/1/1893	Notts County	4–0	Man United
12/11/1892	Man United	1–3	Notts County

FA Cup results

6/2/1904	R1	Notts County	3–3	Man United
10/2/1904	R1r	Man United	3–3	Notts County

MEADOW PAIN

In May 1985 Manchester City brought more than 10,000 fans to Meadow Lane to face County. It was City's penultimate match of the season and a win would have all-but guaranteed them promotion to the First Division.

However, County, battling against relegation to the third tier, raced into a shock 3–0 lead by half time thanks to goals from Justin Fashanu, Rachid Harkouk and Alan Young. During the break, the City fans took things badly and their party mood changed to one of menace as they began to tear down the fences in an attempt to get the game abandoned.

Even pleas from Blues manager Billy McNeill and County boss Jimmy Sirrel failed to quell the travelling masses. When order was finally restored, the match resumed following a 30-minute delay. The 'Pies lost their momentum somewhat after the restart and City pulled two goals back through winger Paul Simpson on 66 and 72 minutes, but County clung on to win 3–2 and earn 3 precious points. The home fans, for their part, were just glad to get away from the ground without further incident. As a footnote, City did win their final game to win promotion, but County failed to get the result they needed against Fulham and were relegated.

GRAB YOUR CRUCIFIX AND GARLIC!

On 1 November 1894 County played perhaps their most unusual friendly match when they took on the ominous-sounding 'Vampires'. The visitors lacked bite and County strolled home 5–2 though rumours that the visitor's keeper didn't like crosses are unconfirmed, as is the myth that the game could only be played at night and the opposition arrived in coffins. Vampires returned for another game two years later, almost to the day, and were losing heavily before coming back (from the dead?) to score three times and lose 7–3. Vampires really went for County's throat in that game – OK – enough bloodsucker jokes! Curiously, one week later County took on Wolves at home with the visiting keeper committing several howlers. Fangs for the memories, eh lads?

JOHN, I'M ONLY BOUNCING

Former County winger John Chiedozie who terrorised defences for the Magpies from 1981 to 1983 moved into the bouncy castle industry after retiring. Well, what else could he do to replace his somewhat inflated wages?

THESE COLOURS DON'T RUN

The Magpies' first recorded club colours were black and amber hoops with records indicating that this was the chosen kit up until 1872. In 1880 County wore chocolate and blue halves and remained the same for the next decade. From then on the more familiar black and white stripes became the norm. Between 1922 and 1926 the club wore white shirts with a black 'V' which included a Magpie on the breast before reverting to stripes again until 1934 when another dabble with chocolate and blue lasted a few games before again reverting to black and white stripes.

In 1946 yet another variation was used with white shirts and black collars and cuffs in a chosen design. The black and white resumed in 1952 for 10 years until white shirts with a black circle round the neck were used for one year. Thereafter the traditional black and white stripes were used.

There is only one occasion on record when County wore not only the colours of another club, but the actual shirts of another team. On 19 November 1949 County travelled to Torquay for a league game without a change of strip and when it was discovered the hosts' shirts clashed with the Magpies', fortunately they were able to borrow Aston Villa's home shirt for the match thanks to a friend of a friend. Though County didn't lose the game they didn't score either – the first time in 17 matches that season.

DO MAGPIES MIGRATE TO AFRICA?

At the end of the 1975/76 campaign, County flew to Africa for a brief tour of Kenya, playing four games in nine days in the country's two biggest cities. The tour was successful on many levels and the Nairobi games saw the 'Pies win both games (Abakubya 2–0 and Gor Mahia 3–1), but the Mombasa matches against Kenya Breweries and Mwenge both ended in defeat, 0–2 and 1–2 respectively.

SVEN SAID IT ...

'I think it's the biggest football challenge of my life, trying to take Notts County back to the Premier League, but that's the target. The challenge is perhaps the most difficult football job I've had so far. But, I am looking forward to it.'

Sven, shortly after arriving at Meadow Lane

'Sol Campbell started training and in the middle of training he went. I don't know if he told the manager he had some small problems. I thought that after training we would have a meeting but when I came back he was gone. He knew the conditions at the club. I'd shown him the ground and the training ground.'

Sven on Sol Campbell's brief County spell

'I am particularly attracted to this role and the unique opportunity to help build a club over the longer term. I started my football management career at a small lower division Swedish club and we managed to get them into the top flight. I can think of no better challenge than to attempt to do that again, but this time with the world's oldest football club.'

Sven on joining the 'Pies

'Sometimes things go wrong in football. You can lose games, own goals, you can buy the wrong players. But you do it in the right spirit and you do it honestly. That is not how it went wrong at Notts County. If you are not trying to cheat people, it is very easy to come out and say that it went wrong.'

Sven on his time at Meadow Lane

TRY AND TRY AGAIN ...

The first Rugby League international to be staged at Meadow Lane was on 12 December 1912 when England took on Australia in a Test match. The result suggests it wasn't the most exciting game, but the 5–3 victory for England was pleasing nonetheless.

NEED THE GOAT

Shaun Goater played just once for Notts County on loan from Rotherham. He later went on to carve a terrific career for himself at Manchester City – but he never forgot his time at Meadow Lane as these quotes from his autobiography, *Feed the Goat*, prove:

'Notts County came in for me. They took me on loan and were in Division Two, a league higher and doing well, too. They had some decent players like Andy Legg and Tony Agana and I made my debut in a 2–1 defeat at Charlton, managing to set up the Notts goal.'

'My second game with Notts County was in the Anglo-Italian Cup against Italian side Brescia and I was suitably impressed – European football in only my second game with them! I had a pre-match meal of pasta and this was probably the first time I'd eaten the right food before a match and I could see Notts County were a well-run outfit and things seemed to be looking up.'

'Before the game with Brescia I received a phone call from the club secretary saying that he'd looked into everything and I wasn't eligible to play in the game – I said 'sorry, what's that?' He told me I couldn't continue my loan with the club because I needed a separate work permit – my current permit only allowed me to play for Rotherham. I couldn't believe it. I was gutted. Hours before I played my first match in Europe and it was taken away from me and, though I didn't know it at the time, that was the nearest I ever got to playing football in European competition.'

ALL AT SEA

The Notts County was a trawler named after the club in the mid-1960s but, perhaps as a portent of future difficulties, the hapless fishing boat sank in Reykjavik harbour several years later!

WAT – NO COUNTY?

Though the Magpies weren't shy of entering doomed cup competitions, they only took part in the innovative Watney Cup on one occasion. The clash with Sheffield United on 29 July 1972 was the only time in the tournament's three-year history that County took part and more is the pity.

The Watney Cup introduced the penalty-shoot-out to these shores and featured live televised matches as well as being the first sponsored football competition. A crowd of 14,405 turned out at Meadow Lane to watch the Blades comprehensively progress to the next round following a 3–0 victory.

LET THERE BE LIGHT – OF SORTS

County took part in a floodlit match for the first time as long ago as 1878 when they played under lights at Bramall Lane, Sheffield. The first floodlit home game, played at Trent Bridge against Derbyshire on 30 November of the same year, had two generators placed behind either goal and the lights suspended on poles shed some light onto the playing area. It was quite innovative for the time, but fate was to conspire against the club and fans when a fog bank obscured play and then one of the generators packed in! More than 4,000 curious locals had turned out to watch County win the game 1–0, but the general consensus was the experiment was quite a way off being fully operational.

CUP PIED

The Magpies became the first Second Division club to win the FA Cup when they romped home to victory in the final against First Division Bolton Wanderers in 1894. However, the Magpies' cup pedigree was good, having reached the final three years earlier only to lose to Blackburn Rovers at the Kennington Oval and having a couple of unsuccessful semi-finals behind them, they were up against some tough sides on the way to the final.

Burnley were the first obstacle the 'Pies overcame with Jimmy Logan's strike enough on the day – despite being reduced to ten men – and Burton Wanderers were dumped out 2–1 in the next round thanks to goals from Donnelly and a Logan penalty. Forest were next up and after a 1–1 draw in the first game, County trounced their rivals 4–1 in the replay. Harry Daft's winner in the semi-final at Bramall Lane, Sheffield, set up a final with Bolton at a Goodison Park packed to the rafters with 37,000 people – many from Nottingham – crammed in, producing record gate receipts of £1,189.

Thousands greeted County on their return to Nottingham with cup fever gripping the city and the normal 5-minute trip back by coach became more like 40 minutes as the throngs of well-wishers sang songs and cheered their heroes along. The Magpies' defence the following year didn't even last to the second round with Sheffield Wednesday winning 5–1 in South Yorkshire.

BEST SEASON

Here is the final league table for County's best-ever top-flight finish, achieved in 1890/91:

		P	W	D	L	F	A	Pts
1	Everton	22	14	1	7	63	29	29
2	Preston NE	22	12	3	7	44	23	27
3	**Notts County**	**22**	**11**	**4**	**7**	**52**	**35**	**26**
4	Wolves	22	12	2	8	39	50	26
5	Bolton W	22	12	1	9	47	34	25
6	Blackburn R	22	11	2	9	52	43	24
7	Sunderland	22	10	5	7	51	31	23
8	Burnley	22	9	3	10	52	63	21
9	Aston Villa	22	7	4	11	45	58	18
10	Accrington	22	6	4	12	28	50	16
11	Derby County	22	7	1	14	47	81	15
12	West Brom	22	5	2	15	34	57	12

HUGHES' HAT-TRICKS

Lee Hughes became the first Notts County player to score more than 30 goals in a season for 60 years when he ended the 2009/10 season with 33 strikes from 44 League Two games. Hughes, who signed on 22 July 2009 scored a hat-trick on his County league debut at home to Bradford City and he added two more before Christmas to enhance his reputation yet further with the supporters. Tommy Lawton achieved a similar feat in 1949/50 when he bagged 33 goals from 40 games.

THE CORINTHIAN SPIRIT

The Corinthians were formed in 1882 and were a kind of amateur all-stars of their day, attracting the best players in the country who would guest for the team before returning to their club sides. County's Harry Cursham represented Corinthians between 1882 and 1886. The first meeting between County and the Corinthians was in 1884 and there were 20 meetings in total up until the final game, played during the 1906/07 campaign. The overall record is:

P: 20   W: 9   D: 3   L: 8   F: 48   A: 46

NO, NOT MAN CITY ... PLEASE!

County fans could be forgiven if they shrieked in fear when their heroes next draw Manchester City in the League Cup. There have only been five meetings in the competition so far but City have won the lot, and usually by a healthy margin. The first meeting at Meadow Lane in 1963 ended 1–0 to City, but the second meeting at Maine Road in 1980 ended 5–1 with City striker Dennis Tueart bagging four for the hosts. In 1998 a two-legged tie began at Meadow Lane with a 2–0 win for City but the second leg was a disaster, ending 7–1! In 2001 the Magpies took on Kevin Keegan's free-scoring City and pushed them all the way into extra time, but the Blues triumphed 4–2 on the night.

Complete record:
P: 5   W: 0   D: 0   L: 5   F: 4   A: 19

CAMPBELL'S MEATBALLS

Sol Campbell was County's biggest signing ever – but he played just one game before controversially quitting Meadow Lane after feeling he'd been misled, somewhat – here are his thoughts on that infamous departure.

'I'm not embarrassed, not hurt or humbled or anything like that – I am just disappointed. I bought into a dream and I wanted to make that dream a reality. But it took me less than a month to realise that it was all heading to a different conclusion.'

Sol, conscience clear

'I knew I would be the club's first big signing but was told I would be the first of many. Names like Roberto Carlos and Benjani were mentioned. But nothing materialised.'

Sol feels lonely without other big stars to keep him company

'That's nonsense. I'm not a prima donna. I'm from Stratford, East London. I can get down and dirty. I just roll my sleeves up and get on with it. Let's be honest – I knew the standard of football was going to be dramatically different from the Premier League. And as for the trip to Morecambe, the facilities at Morecambe, they weren't actually that bad. I've seen worse. Remember, I used to be at Portsmouth – have you seen Fratton Park? Have you been to the training ground?'

Sol responds to suggestions he didn't fancy the facilities in League Two

HIGHS AND LOWS

The Magpies' post-war attendances have fluctuated greatly over the years. Here is a record of the benchmark biggest gates of the season, plus the games the people of Nottingham gave a wide berth to in that particular year! Of the 66 seasons since the war, Forest have been the star attraction on twelve occasions, with the nearest team after that being Mansfield Town with six top crowds.

Season	Highest Crowd		Lowest Crowd	
2009/10	11,331	v Cheltenham	4,606	v Darlington
2008/09	6,686	v Rotherham Utd	2,886	v Luton Town
2007/08	10,027	v Mansfield Town	3,421	v Darlington
2006/07	10,034	v Mansfield Town	3,010	v Barnet
2005/06	9,817	v Bury	3,710	v Wycombe W
2004/05	10,055	v Mansfield Town	3,586	v Macclesfield
2003/04	9,601	v Sheffield Wed	4,145	v Brentford
2002/03	10,302	v Mansfield Town	3,875	v Crewe Alex
2001/02	15,618	v Huddersfield	3,140	v Colchester
2000/01	9,125	v Stoke City	2,860	v Colchester
1999/2000	9,677	v Stoke City	3,728	v Oldham Ath
1998/99	10,316	v Manchester City	3,294	v Wrexham
1997/98	12,430	v Rotherham Utd	3,104	v Chester City
1996/97	6,879	v Preston NE	2,423	v Plymouth A
1995/96	8,725	v Swindon Town	3,462	v York City
1994/95	11,102	v Sheffield United	4,703	v Tranmere R
1993/94	17,911	v Forest	5,302	v Oxford Utd
1992/93	14,841	v Newcastle Utd	5,037	v Cambridge Utd
1991/92	21,055	v Man Utd	6,198	v Wimbledon
1990/91	15,546	v Sheffield Wed	5,086	v Charlton Ath
1989/90	10,151	v Bristol Rovers	4,586	v Brentford
1988/89	11,590	v Sheffield Utd	3,940	v Swansea City
1987/88	8,854	v Sunderland	4,044	v Bury

Season	Highest Crowd	Lowest Crowd
1986/87	8,820 v Mansfield Town	3,409 v Bristol Rovers
1985/86	13,086 v Derby County	2,345 v Darlington
1984/85	17,812 v Manchester City	3,409 v Charlton Ath
1983/84	18,745 v Liverpool	5,378 v Wolverhampton W
1982/83	23,552 v Forest	5,846 v Southampton
1981/82	19,304 v Forest	6,707 v Middlesbrough
1980/81	16,560 v Derby Co	6,565 v Oldham Athletic
1979/80	14,849 v Leicester City	5,505 v Orient
1978/79	21,571 v Stoke City	4,374 v Wrexham
1977/78	15,718 v Bolton W	7,200 v Blackpool
1976/77	32,518 v Forest	7,845 v Charlton Ath
1975/76	29,279 v Forest	8,005 v Carlisle United
1974/75	20,303 v Forest	7,227 v Bristol City
1973/74	32,310 v Forest	6,975 v Cardiff City
1972/73	23,613 v Tranmere Rovers	6,118 v Swansea City
1971/72	34,208 v Aston Villa	8,921 v Torquay United
1970/71	21,012 v Northampton T	5,826 v Barrow
1969/70	15,346 v Chesterfield	2,456 v Northampton T
1968/69	9,801 v Chesterfield	3,089 v Chester
1967/68	9,990 v Chesterfield	3,741 v Exeter City
1966/67	6,491 v Southport	2,919 v Crewe Alex
1965/66	7,388 v Darlington	1,927 v Chesterfield
1964/65	8,460 v Darlington	3,219 v Rochdale
1963/64	18,669 v Coventry City	2,640 v Bournemouth
1962/63	14,320 v Port Vale	3,455 v Carlisle United
1961/62	19,466 v Peterborough Utd	3,688 v Hull City
1960/61	26,759 v Coventry City	3,933 v Brentford
1959/60	22,788 v Walsall	8,793 v Gateshead
1958/59	16,510 v Mansfield Town	4,359 v Brentford
1957/58	23,966 v Derby County	9,942 v Bristol City
1956/57	42,489 v Leicester City	4,869 v Grimsby Town
1955/56	25,622 v Leicester City	9,563 v Fulham
1954/55	31,018 v Forest	10,395 v Luton Town

Season	Highest Crowd	Lowest Crowd
1953/54	36,929 v Forest	9,971 v West Ham Utd
1952/53	39,920 v Forest	7,529 v Everton
1951/52	44,087 v Forest	13,161 v Rotherham Utd
1950/51	44,195 v Preston NE	13,873 v Manchester City
1949/50	46,000 v Forest	27,076 v Aldershot
1948/49	36,615 v Exeter City	19,478 v Brighton & HA
1947/48	45,116 v Swansea Town	14,065 v Bournemouth
1946/47	28,450 v Cardiff City	6,142 v Reading

THEY SAID IT ...

'Don't send him off, ref – there will be nothing left in our pockets when we get back in the dressing room.'

Legendary County keeper Albert Iremonger was never short of a quip

'I can't just pick one happy memory of my time with Notts County as there have been so many. It's been fantastic. I've probably been through every emotion you can possibly imagine. Obviously knowing we'd won the championship after the game away at Darlington was fantastic. Beating Wigan away from home in the FA Cup was amazing as well. But over the course of this season there have been a lot of highs.'

Kasper Schmeichel on the good times

'It's a bit of a weird feeling, leaving the club. I'm excited about my prospects and what could happen, but there's also a degree of sadness. I've enjoyed my time here and I'll definitely miss the place, the players and the fans, but it's one of those things and there's no other way it can be. I just have to take it on the chin and move on really. I'll follow Notts forever, always look for their results and come back and visit a few times.'

Kasper Schmeichel on departing Meadow Lane

'It will be a massive blow if he leaves because he has been brilliant since he came in. As soon as he stepped through the door I knew he would be a good manager and we would do really well under him. He got the best out of us and we went on a great run to win the title. If he leaves he would go with all of our best wishes because he has been a different class for us.'

**Ben Davies prior to Steve Cotterill's
departure in 2010**

'It has been a real pleasure working with such a fantastic group of people from the chairman and chief executive, players, the backroom staff, office workers and ground staff. The fans have been magnificent to me and I would like to thank everyone connected with the club for how they have received me since I've been here and wish them all the very best in the future.'

**Steve Cotterill shortly after confirming his departure
from Meadow Lane**

'The opening of the Nottingham Football Club commenced on Tuesday last at Cremorne Gardens. A side was chosen by W. Arkwright and Chas Deakin. A very spirited game resulted in the latter scoring two goals and two rogues against one and one.'

The *Nottingham Guardian*, 1862

THE TRAGIC TALE OF CUP FINAL HERO JIMMY LOGAN

Jimmy Logan, hero of the 1893/94 FA Cup triumph, met an untimely end through a series of oversights. Logan scored a hat-trick in the final against Bolton Wanderers at Goodison Park to help County to a 4–1 win, but within two years, he was dead. Logan left Nottingham in 1894 and played for Dundee and Newcastle before moving on to Loughborough. On a trip to play Newton Heath in Manchester, their kit was mislaid and despite efforts to find a replacement, the team had to play in their normal day shirts. As often seems to happen in Manchester, it rained during the game and with no change of clothes, the players wore their damp attire on the train back home. Unfortunately for Logan, he caught a chill and despite initially shaking it off and scoring in the final game of the season against Crewe, he relapsed shortly after and developed full-blown pneumonia. In May 1896, he died aged just 25.

NOTTS COUNTY'S HIGHEST FINISH

Notts County have never won the top division title, but they came fairly close on a couple of occasions. The Magpies finished third in 1891 and 1901, but no higher unfortunately. In 1983/84 County topped the table – after just two games! The highest top-flight finish of modern times was 15th in 1982/83.

HARRY WASN'T DAFT

Harry Daft scored 80 goals in 176 games for the Magpies during two spells with the club and represented England 5 times, scoring 3 goals. Son of legendary cricketer, Richard, Harry could also bat, too. He managed 4,370 runs during his first-class career for Nottinghamshire and was bowled out on his debut by the great W.G. Grace, no less. In all he also took 86 wickets and 81 catches.

SWEET SIXTEEN

County's longest consecutive spell in the top division was from 1897 to 1913 when the Magpies enjoyed sixteen seasons of football at the highest level. In fact, the club spent the first 38 years of the Football League in reasonably good shape, never leaving the top two divisions until relegation to the nation's third division in 1930.

ON THE UP

Notts have won promotion on thirteen occasions all told. On three occasions they entered Division One as champions (1896/97, 1913/14 and 1922/23) and the latest vault up the leagues was in 2009/10 when the 'Pies achieved promotion in some style.

TESTING TIMES ...

Despite winning the Second Division in 1896/97, the system agreed meant a four-game decider to determine promotion. In the sequence of games, called 'Test matches', County beat Sunderland 1–0 at home and drew 0–0 away before drawing 1–1 with Burnley at home and winning the return 1–0 to top the mini-league and secure promotion to the top flight. The Magpies had previously failed to be promoted after successive Test match failures (sort of early forerunners of the play-off finals) in 1893/94 and 1894/95, so some justice was seen to have been done, though the whole format caused enough complaints to see the end of the injustice in 1899.

DID YOU KNOW?

Notts County are the only English club whose correct name is an abbreviation (Notts for Nottinghamshire). Other possibles could have been Northants Town, Leics City and Yorks City – but none of them run off the tongue like Notts, do they?

TRANSFER FEES

County's first four-figure transfer fee was in October 1912 when they paid £1,500 for Tottenham's Jimmy Cantrell. The 'Pies then set a British record in 1947 when they paid Chelsea £20,000 for the services of the legendary Tommy Lawton – a major shock at the time because County were in Division Three (South) (think of Wayne Rooney signing for Bristol Rovers!) The British record was again broken by County in 1951 when £34,500 was shelled out for Jackie Sewell.

Tony Agana cost £750,000 when he moved to Meadow Lane from Sheffield United in November 1991, though the fee Sven-Goran Eriksson paid Manchester City for Kasper Schmeichel in 2009 is believed to have been greater – but with the fee being undisclosed, we can only guess at the actual figure paid.

The most County have received for a player is £2.5m in 1992 when Derby County took Craig Short – now manager at Meadow Lane – to the Baseball Ground.

ENGLAND UNDER-21

Four County players have represented England at Under-21 level over the years. Brian Kilcline won the first of his three caps in 1982 and another defender, Dean Yates won five caps in 1989 while Tommy Johnson (5) and Mark Draper (3) won theirs between 1991 and 1992.

PULLING OUR LEGG?

Eat your heart out Rory Delap – long throw-ins were a staple of life at Meadow Lane during Andy Legg's spell with County. The County defender was entered into the *Guinness Book of World Records* with a throw measuring 41.6 metres. His personal best – though unofficial – is a whopping 46.5 metres!

THE DON SPEAKS ...

Don Masson was one of the Magpies' greatest servants and was voted best player of all-time on a recent poll. Here are some quotes from the great man himself:

'Unlike now, most of the players would have played for nothing. I came from a little village in Scotland and all I wanted to do was play football. To play for Scotland was beyond my wildest dreams. I would give up all the money I have now and the lifestyle to go back and play football. I didn't realise I was given a gift to be able to do that – you take it for granted at the time. When you look back, you think, "Crikey, how lucky was I to do that?"'

'My penalty miss against Peru in the 1978 World Cup finals was probably my career low. We had such a good team at the time and had I scored I think we might have gone on to qualify for the next round. It was a nice height and the goalkeeper anticipated it, so fair play to him. It took me a long time to recover from it. If I had not done that, people would not have remembered me after all these years. At least I think they have forgiven me now!'

'The worst thing about being a footballer in the seventies was going out at night and getting hassled by supporters from other teams, mostly drunken ones. That was part and parcel of the game because we used to go into pubs and mix with the fans. We didn't think we were anything special because we kicked a silly football about. Nowadays the players are cocooned away from the supporters.'

'My most difficult opponent was, without doubt, Gerry Gow. He kicked me all over the place. He was at Bristol City, who were in the First Division, and used to man-mark me. I knew when we played them it was going to be a nightmare. He used to ignore the ball. He said, "I've been told to mark you and I'm going to kick you all day." I dreaded playing against him. He made my life a misery.'

'I can remember travelling down to London with my Notts County boss, Jimmy Sirrel, to complete the transfer. Jimmy said beforehand "Make sure you don't sign when you go in there." He didn't mention at that point that there were other clubs lined up to speak to me. But as soon as I saw the Queen's Park Rangers manager Dave Sexton and he told me what his plans for the club were, I shook hands on the deal straight away. All the other players at Loftus Road were full internationals so it was a great move for me. Then when we were going back to Nottingham on the train afterwards, Jimmy Sirrel said: "What did you sign for little fellow? I could have got Southampton – they were in for you. And Don Revie at Leeds United wanted you too."'

STRANGER DANGER

The first recorded clash between County and Nottingham Forest was on 22 March 1866 when the eleven men of Notts took on the seventeen of Forest! With rules still in their embryonic stage and pretty much anything going, the game ended 0–0. A return game was arranged just under a month later and this time it was ten Forest players against eleven Notts players and it again ended 0–0. Interestingly, one of County's number was listed by a match reporter in the local press as 'A Stranger' – seeing as there are records of such a surname, we must assume the player was indeed a stranger – at least to the guy writing the article!

TWO FOR JOY?

The only other English league club nicknamed the Magpies are Newcastle United, though County are the only one to have the bird (actually two in total) on the official club crest. Because our club was formed way before the Geordies, it's our nickname – so back off!

FIRST SUB

Substitutes were first introduced during the 1965/66 season, but County's first replacement from the bench wasn't used until 5 February when Dennis Shiels replaced Brian Bates during the 2–1 home win over Lincoln City. It's believed that County were the last team in the top flight to actually use the option of a sub for some unknown reason.

SHANKS FOR NOTHING!

Notts County never faced a Liverpool side managed by Bill Shankly. The legendary Liverpool boss was in the Anfield hot seat from December 1959 until July 1974 – but the Magpies didn't play the Merseysiders from 1958 until 1982 so were never able to sample the great man's wit in person.

DAFT DEVILS

Harry Daft's testimonial match against Derby County on 8 November 1894 resulted in a 6–0 victory for the Rams at Trent Bridge – hardly a happy day for Harry, apart from the attendance purse he was handed at the end of the game, of course.

PLAY-OFFS

Neil Warnock guided County to successive promotions via the play-off finals in 1990 and 1991. The Magpies went from Division Three to the top tier over the course of two years, ensuring Warnock would always be popular at Meadow Lane. On the first occasion, the Magpies saw off Bolton Wanderers in the semi-final before beating Tranmere Rovers 2–0 at Wembley in front of 29,252 fans.

The following season County edged two keenly contested semi-final legs against Middlesbrough to win through and earn the right to take on Brighton & Hove Albion. Two goals from Tommy Johnson and another from former West Brom legend Cyrille Regis gave Warnock's men a memorable 3–1 victory in front of just shy of 60,000 fans. On the flip side, County have also twice suffered disappointment in the play-offs.

In 1988 Walsall won 3–1 at Meadow Lane in the first leg of the semi-final and the second leg ended 1–1, meaning a 4–2 aggregate defeat. In 1996, after seeing Crewe off 3–2 on aggregate in the semis, County lost 2–0 to Bradford City in the final – you can't win 'em all!

SHORT AND SHARP

Craig Short became County's manager in 2010 – here are a couple of thoughts on the appointment from the man himself, and Mr Warnock:

'I am delighted that the chairman is prepared to give a hungry young manager a chance and I feel that I have shown the desire to succeed here. If I can enjoy half as much success here as a manager as I did as a player, it's going to be a fantastic time for myself and the club.'

Craig Short

'He was probably not the favourite for the job. But I told him to be himself, because they would see what he is all about and that he loves Notts County, and they clearly have. The club's board has to take a lot of credit because they were not swayed by the reputation of some of the other people who wanted it – they have gone for a young, hungry manager – and the right man.'

Neil Warnock

UNWANTED RECORD

The Magpies hold a rather unwanted English record, but one that we're stuck with all the same. Between 2002 and 2003 the club were in financial administration for a total of 534 days. During the process of wild boardroom upheaval, the club was briefly run by Albert Scardino, a Pulitzer prize-winning journalist and one of Bill Clinton's press aides!

WHAT GOES UP?

When it comes to yo-yoing through the divisions, County take some beating. With a total of thirteen promotions and fifteen relegations up to 2010, no club has moved between the divisions of the Football League on more occasions than the 'Pies. The club went up in 1897, 1914,

1923, 1931, 1950, 1960, 1971, 1973, 1981, 1990, 1991, 1998 and 2010. The relegation years were 1893, 1913, 1920, 1926, 1930, 1935, 1958, 1959, 1964, 1984, 1985, 1992, 1995, 1997 and 2004.

GREAT DANE

Kasper Schmeichel kept an incredible 26 clean sheets during County's record-breaking 2009/10 campaign and was one of the main reasons the 'Pies escaped the bottom division. Unfortunately, that drew unwanted attention from bigger clubs further up the leagues. Kasper, hugely popular at Meadow Lane, left the club at the end of the 2009/10 campaign and signed for Championship side Leeds United.

THE FOURTH KIND

When County win the fourth tier of English football, they usually do it in style. In 2009/10 the Magpies won League Two by winning 27 of their 46 games and ending with a +65 goal difference. During 1997/98 County won 10 successive league games and won 29 of their 46 games. Jimmy Sirrel's Notts won 30 of their 46 games in 1970/71 and remained unbeaten at home. The only other occasion in which County were promoted from the bottom division was in 1959/60, when they finished as runners-up.

UP FOR THE CUP

County are somewhat overdue an FA Cup triumph – not that it's likely to come any time soon if we're realistic. The Magpies' one and only success was in 1894 where a little bit of history was created as County were outside the top flight at the time they beat Bolton Wanderers 4–1 in the final. Jimmy Logan scored a hat-trick in the victory and County became the first team outside the top flight to win the trophy.

County reached the final in 1891 but went down 3–1 to Blackburn Rovers and the only other high point of an otherwise decidedly average record was a semi-final appearance in 1922. The last sniff of Wembley was in 2010 when County reached the last sixteen of the competition, though you needed a strong sense of smell to be aware of it.

MOST APPEARANCES – TOP 10

	Name	Career	Appearances
1	Albert Iremonger	1904–26	601
2	Brian Stubbs	1968–80	486
3	Pedro Richards	1974–86	485
4	David Needham	1965–77	471
5	Don Masson	1968–82	455
6	Les Bradd	1967–78	442
7	Percy Mills	1927–39	434
8=	Billy Flint	1908–26	408
8=	David Hunt	1977–87	408
10	Dean Yates	1985–95	394

MOST GOALS – TOP 10

Les Bradd is County's all-time top goalscorer with 137 strikes in 11 years. Although Tony Hateley only ended 23 goals adrift of his former team-mate, there is no suggestion that Bradd's record will be overtaken any time soon.

	Name	Career	Goals
1	Les Bradd	1967–78	137
2	Tony Hateley	1958–63, 1970–72	114
3	Jackie Sewell	1946–51	104
4	Tommy Lawton	1947–52	103
5	Tom Keetley	1929–33	98
6	Don Masson	1968–82	97
7	Tom Johnston	1948–57	93
8	Ian McParland	1980–89	90
9	Harry Daft	1885–95	81
10=	Mark Stallard	1999–2004, 2005	79
10=	Trevor Christie	1979–84	79
10=	Gary Lund	1987–95	79

NOT UP FOR (THIS) CUP

Notts County have never gone beyond the quarter-final stage of the League Cup, reaching the last eight on three occasions in 1963/64, 1972/73 and 1975/76. It's not a competition the Magpies fans look forward to with any great relish or expectation, it has to be said.

THE ITALIAN JOB

Where the Magpies have failed in other competitions, they have done particularly well in at least one other that is slightly off the radar of Arsenal and Chelsea. OK, it may not be the Champions League, but the Anglo-Italian Cup will always hold a fond place in the County fans' hearts, and with good reason, too. In 1992/93 the Magpies began their first foray in the competition, losing 4–2 to Derby County and then drawing 1–1 at home to Barnsley in the group stage, ending interest for that season.

With a new-found taste for pasta and olive oil, County returned a year later to avenge Derby 3–2 and then to hold Nottingham Forest 1–1 to progress to the First Round group stage where they faced four Italian sides. County proved more than a match for their Latin cousins, beating Ascoli 4–2 at Meadow Lane, followed by a 3–2 home win over Pisa. Despite a 3–1 reverse to Brescia, County then went to Ancona and left with a 1–0 win. That meant a semi-final with the very Italian (not) Southend United over two legs. Both matches ended 1–0 to the home teams, meaning a penalty shoot-out at Meadow Lane with County winning 4–3 to earn a place at Wembley. However, on 20 March 1994 they met their nemesis Brescia again and in front of 17,185 fans, the Italians scored the only goal of the game to win the cup.

County learned from the previous year's exploits to go one better in the next campaign. Though three of their four group games ended in draws, County secured a 1–0 win over Lecce to progress to a two-legged semi-final with Stoke City. The Potters left Meadow Lane with a satisfying 0–0 draw, but County ground out a similarly pleasing draw in the return leg, meaning a second successive penalty shoot-out for the right to play in a Wembley final, though the DVD sales of both legs didn't exactly fly off the shelves! Just as they had the year before, County edged through in a 5-goal thriller – 3–2 – to have another crack at bringing an all-too-rare piece of silverware back to Nottingham. Standing in their way were Serie B side Ascoli, but they were brushed aside by goals from Agana and White which gave the Magpies a 2–1 win in front of a disappointing 11,704 fans.

JUVE COPYCATS

The 'Old Lady' of Italian football owes their famous back and white striped kit to the Magpies. Juventus have played in the strip – sometimes with white shorts, sometimes with black shorts – since 1903, though they originally played in pink shirts with a black tie (!) which had only occurred due to the wrong shirts being sent to the club in the first place. After the kits were washed to the point of falling apart, club officials sought to replace them. One of their team members, Englishman John Savage, was asked if he had any contacts in England who could supply new shirts in a colour that would better withstand the elements. He had a friend who lived in Nottingham, who being a Notts County supporter, shipped out the black and white striped shirts to Turin – the rest, as they say, is history.

DOUBLE FIGURES

County's record victory in any form came way back in 1885 when Rotherham were dispatched in style, returning to South Yorkshire with their tails firmly between their legs following a 15–0 FA Cup first round thrashing at Trent Bridge. Notts' assault on the same part of Britain continued with an 8–0 win over Sheffield in the next round. The Magpies' biggest league win was an 11–1 win over Newport County at Meadow Lane in Division Three (South) on 15 January 1949. Notts' last major win of any kind was a 15–1 win over Newquay in July 2002, though this was only a friendly.

ALL-TIME FAVOURITE PLAYER: DON MASSON

Yes, beating even the great Tommy Lawton, when a national poll was carried out during the 2007/08 campaign, County fans voted in their thousands for great Scottish midfielder Don Masson.

Masson was a true club legend, blessed with incredible vision and a broad range of passing. Perhaps the most important thing to the fans who voted for him was that Masson was incredibly loyal to the Magpies, despite plenty of interest from other clubs over the years. His best years were all spent at Meadow Lane and, had he been with a more successful club, who knows how brightly his star might have shone?

He'd been a County player for six years when he left for QPR in 1976, helping the Hoops to within a few points of the league title in the process. He stayed with QPR for two years, becoming a huge crowd favourite there too, and then went to Derby County before returning to Nottingham for four years more with County.

Masson captained County to three promotions, from the Fourth Division right the way through to the top flight, and in that time, he made 402 league appearances and scored 92 goals – the mark of genuine club great. His 17 caps for Scotland were scant reward for his efforts at club level and manager Billy Gray's decision to bring him to the club from Middlesbrough in 1968 for a fee of £6,000 (along with Bob Worthington), was perhaps the best piece of business ever conducted by a County boss.

He won the Player of the Year award a record three times during his time at Meadow Lane, and it was fitting that after his final game for County at home to Manchester United in 1982, he decided to hang his boots up for good.

GOLDEN GATE

The highest gate receipts County ever received were for the 1991 FA Cup sixth round tie with Manchester City. Swelled by more than 8,000 travelling fans, Notts raked in £124,539 on the day – and won 1–0 thanks to a last-gasp Gary Lund goal. The record, although almost 20 years old, still stands today.

COUNTY – CHAMPIONS OF EUROPE!

County effectively became Europe's number one team – of sorts – when they opened the 1981/82 campaign with a 1–0 away win to Aston Villa. They repeated the victory by the same score at Meadow Lane. A few months later Villa won the European Cup – surely making County superior force in Europe? Well they did beat the European champions home and away . . . no? Well, worth a try!

DANISH BACON

County's first ever overseas tour took place in June 1910 when, having accepted a guarantee of £200 from Akademisk Boldklub, they travelled over to take on a Danish XI and won two of the three games, drawing the other. The Magpies returned to Denmark in 1923, beating a Copenhagen XI 3–0 and again 1–0, before taking on their old foes, the Danish XI, 3–2.

COUNTY v CLOUGHIE

The Magpies took on neighbours Nottingham Forest in the Trentside derby under Brian Clough's tenure on fourteen occasions in league and cup competitions. Forest have almost always been in the ascendency during that period, but despite this, the 'Pies have a more than respectable record against a side who were league champions and twice crowned champions of Europe during the 17-year spell. In fact, Cloughie had to wait until his sixth attempt before finally getting the better of County who beat his team on four occasions and held them to a draw another five times.

The Clough Years record is:

P: 14   W: 4   D: 5   L: 5   F: 15   A: 22

1991/92	11 Jan	Forest 1–1 County	First Division
1991/92	24 Aug	County 0–4 Forest	First Division
1983/84	31 Mar	County 0–0 Forest	First Division

1983/84	16 Oct	Forest 3–1 County	First Division
1982/83	23 Apr	Forest 2–1 County	First Division
1982/83	4 Dec	County 3–2 Forest	First Division
1981/82	12 Apr	County 1–2 Forest	First Division
1981/82	23 Jan	Forest 0–2 County	First Division
1977/78	25 Oct	Forest 4–0 County	League Cup
1976/77	9 Apr	County 1–1 Forest	Second Division
1976/77	8 Mar	Forest 1–2 County	Second Division
1975/76	13 Apr	County 0–0 Forest	Second Division
1975/76	30 Aug	Forest 0–1 County	Second Division
1974/75	25 Mar	County 2–2 Forest	Second Division

NOT SO WELCOME, MATT?

Former Sky Sports presenter Matt Lorenzo was appointed Head of Communications at Notts County FC in 2009 but resigned after just two weeks in the role. No explanation was forthcoming.

MORE QUOTES ...

'I always said that I wanted to come back to the Premier League. I have chosen a difficult way to do it. It will take some years, but we will do it. We are starting from almost the bottom of the bottom so it is maybe the biggest football challenge in my life to take this club to the Premier League, but that is the target. I'm here for that challenge, and that is the truth.'

Sven-Goran Eriksson on his shock appointment at Meadow Lane

'I know a lot of agents and they are already phoning from half of Europe. I'll have to switch it off.'

Sven, always well-connected – except if you call his phone . . .

'I know the teams, but not how they play. I have to do some homework quickly.'

Sven admits he hasn't a clue whether Northampton – or anyone else outside the Premier League for that matter – play a diamond formation

'Milan have made me aware that they want me to go back there, play there and train there, and I'm more than happy with that. I have got other options, though. Once I have time to decide, I will. Clubs have made offers already, three or four of them. But not Notts County. I haven't spoken to Sven for a while.'

David Beckham weighs up the options at the San Siro or Meadow Lane!

'It was a fantastic night for everyone involved. The lads were very disciplined and when they did break through, Kasper was there to make some great saves. It makes us all very proud. I'm just here, keeping things going, and if the investment comes in, I'm pretty sure there'll be a new manager.'

Caretaker boss Dave Kevan after a 2–2 draw with Premier League Wigan Athletic in the League Cup

'We've got more fans than you!'

The travelling County fans taunt the Wigan supporters during a League Cup tie – at Wigan!

HOW LOW CAN YOU GO?

County have twice finished 21st in the nation's fourth division – worryingly both in recent years! In 2005/06 and two years later in 2007/08, the Magpies almost slipped out of the Football League altogether, with a draw with Bury in 2006 helping preserve league status.

CALL 911!

Notts County's heaviest defeat has occurred on three occasions and all within a 40-year period. On 29 September 1888 Aston Villa won 9–1 and just over a year later Blackburn Rovers repeated the dose. Portsmouth were the last team to join the 9–1 club, pummelling County on 9 April 1927 at Fratton Park. In the 1990s, County suffered a couple of 7–1 defeats, firstly at home to Newcastle in 1993 and then at Manchester City in August 1998. While all three 9–1 losses were in the league, the 7–1 thrashings were both in the League Cup.

JUMP LEEDS

Leeds United delivered the kind of opening day nightmare most clubs dread but few actually suffer. On the first day of the 1953/54 season, County, who had just survived relegation on the final day of the previous campaign, were beaten 6–0 at Elland Road. Stung by the thrashing, County were again involved in a six-goal game in their next match, a 3–3 draw at Bury. Later in the season, Notts restored some pride by beating Leeds 2–0 at Meadow Lane in the return fixture.

HIGHEST CROWD

Meadow Lane's biggest gate was for the March 1955 visit of York City. A crowd of 47,310 crammed in to watch the FA Cup sixth round tie, but the majority went home disappointed after the visitors left with a 1–0 win.

YOUNGEST PLAYER

Tony Bircumshaw was just 16 years and 54 days old when he made his debut for Notts on 3 April 1961. His older brother played in the same game, which ended in a 3–0 defeat to Brentford. Tony played the next day too, once again against Brentford, but enjoyed his home debut slightly more after a 0–0 draw at Meadow Lane.

RIVALS

It goes without saying that Nottingham Forest are County's oldest and fiercest rivals, but geography demands there are several others, too. Games against Nottinghamshire neighbours Mansfield Town always stir up emotions, as do clashes with Derby County, Leicester City, Burton Albion, Lincoln City and Chesterfield. For reasons other than geography, clashes with Luton Town have taken on a bit of an edge over the years with a victory over the Hatters always sweet.

MORE SEQUENCES

Fewest wins in a season
Though there have been a couple of occasions when County have won just five games in a campaign, they were when the league had far fewer teams in each division. In modern times, County won just 7 games out of 46 during the 1996/97 season, which is the worst in modern times.

Most defeats in a season
County suffered 28 losses during 1963/64 and lost all but 3 of their away games. Not surprisingly, the Magpies were relegated and finished bottom – a campaign best forgotten, in fact!

Fewest goals scored in a season
The worst goal drought the club has suffered was 28 in 1912/13. County had failed to score in 20 of their 38 games that season and the top scorer was Peart with 7 – all scored in the final 11 games of the campaign. Just 33 goals in 46 games were managed in 1996/97.

Most goals conceded in a season
In 1934/35, relegated County shipped 97 goals during a truly forgettable season – the tally was 101 if you include the 4–0 drubbing by Wolves in the FA Cup.

Fewest home wins
The 2–1 home win over Blackburn Rovers during the 1904/05 season proved to be the only victory in 17 league fixtures at Meadow Lane as County finished bottom of Division One. Coupled with the failure to win the first two games of the following season, the club's worst run at home of one win in 19 was etched into the record books.

Fewest away wins

Just one victory has been recorded on the road on no less than six occasions, most recently in 1977/78. Interestingly (and thankfully), the Magpies have never endured an entire season without winning an away game.

Most draws in a season

The 'Pies have twice drawn 18 matches during one season – the first in 1968/69 and the second time was in 2007/08.

SHEFFIELD STEAL

Though County are the oldest professional football club in the world, Sheffield FC are the oldest surviving club (having been formed in 1857, five years before Notts came into being). As they were neither United or Wednesday at the time, County are without doubt the oldest recognisable club in the world, though. Besides, Sheffield pretty much made their own rules up and the game they played barely resembled football as we know it at all.

JUST NOT CRICKET!

Though the Magpies played plenty of games at Trent Bridge, there were occasions when the football and cricket seemed to become intermingled – how else can one explain County outscoring Nottinghamshire CCC on one occasion? While Notts County thrashed Rotherham United 15–0 in 1885 – literally running up a cricket score – Yorkshire bowled Notts all out for just 13 in 1901. To date, sanity has been restored and County have never again managed to outscore their cricketing neighbours since.

'PIES v BARCA

Whisper it quietly, but Notts County are a team Barcelona have never beaten. True, the teams met a long time ago and there wasn't so much of a hint of a Lionel Messi or a Zlatan Ibrahimovic back then, but the fact is County have played Barca five times, all in Spain, and won four and drawn one. All the games were played at the Catalonians' first stadium, Camp de la Indústria, which had a capacity of just 8,000. Having won promotion to Division One, the club celebrated with a trip to Spain and organised three friendlies in May and June 1914. It involved a gruelling non-stop 39-hour trip by coach and ferry and the team were greeted by a baked-hard, grassless pitch.

The Magpies won the first game 3–1, won the second 4–2 and cruised home in the final match of the mini-tour 10–3. Incredibly, the Magpies had been 2–1 down at the break but came back to score nine goals in the second period – yes, that was *nine* goals in one half. During the visit, several members of the squad had taken in a bullfight, but left the spectacle feeling disgusted with the whole affair. Eight years later County returned to Spanish soil where they first took on another touring side, St Mirren, and lost 2–1. Next up were back-to-back games with Barca, the first of which was won 4–2. County drew the second game 1–1 before returning to England. So, tell your friends and anyone else that will listen and eat your heart out Arsenal, Manchester United and Chelsea!

County's overall record against one of the greatest clubs in the world is:

P: 5   W: 4   D: 1   L: 0   F: 22   A: 9

APPEARANCES

Goalkeeping legend Albert Iremonger made 564 league and 37 FA Cup appearances during his 21-year career with County and once enjoyed a run of 211 consecutive league starts. No wonder the 'Pies struggled to attract a reserve keeper.

YOUNGEST PLAYER – ALL COMPS

Jermaine Pennant came on as a sub in a Football League Trophy tie at home to Hull City on 22 December 1998, and was just 13 days short of his 16th birthday when he came on as a substitute in the FA Cup tie at Sheffield United on 2 January 1999.

ROCK ON, TOMMY:
QUOTES ABOUT TOMMY LAWTON

'Don't think too much of yourself. You've a long way to go and a lot to learn.'

Alick Robinson, Burnley skipper after Lawton's double-strike in only his second ever league game

'He's not to see the papers. Take out the sports page and throw it on the fire.'

Burnley coach Billy Dougall advises Tommy's grandfather after his two goals against Swansea capture the headlines

'I know you've come here to take my place. Anything I can do to help you I will. I promise – anything at all.'

Dixie Dean, Everton

'No hesitation, no nerves, just the work of a truly great player, a natural goalscorer.'

Billy Wright

'Technically, surely he was the greatest number nine of all time.'

Joe Mercer

'You'll be no bloody good at this heading lark 'til you move your feet more.'

Dixie Dean again

'With Tommy I could guarantee he would make contact with nine out of ten crosses.'

The legendary Stanley Matthews

'Lawton and Dean used to work together under the main stand, Dean throwing up a large cased ball, stuffed with wet paper to make it as heavy as a medicine ball.'

Gordon Watson, ex-Everton

'Well, that's it then. That's the swan song. That's the end of it.'

Dixie Dean realises his time at Everton is coming to an end after a brilliant goal by Lawton – and tells team-mate Joe Mercer as much!

JUSTIN TIME

Justin Fashanu became Britain's first black £1million pound player when he joined Nottingham Forest from Norwich City in 1981. His time at the City Ground wasn't happy and despite his huge price tag, he was allowed to join County in 1982 for just £150,000. Fashanu was a hit at Meadow Lane, staying for three seasons and scoring 20 goals in 64 league appearances. Justin's personal life made his career doubly difficult, particularly when he admitted to being gay. Sadly, Justin took his own life in 1998 following accusations regarding his personal life and two decades after he first came out of the closet, he remains the only professional footballer to have done so. Whichever way you look at it, Justin was, in his own way, a courageous young man.

CLUB FIRSTS

County had to wait until 1888 to begin their first Football League season. There was only one division to begin with and it was Preston North End who won the title, dropping just 4 points all season. The Magpies finished second from bottom!

Here is the 1888/89 table:

	Pld	W	D	L	F	A	Pts
Preston North End	22	18	4	0	74	15	40
Aston Villa	22	12	5	5	61	43	29
Wolves	22	12	4	6	50	37	28
Blackburn Rovers	22	10	6	6	66	45	26
Bolton Wanderers	22	10	2	10	63	59	22
West Brom A	22	10	2	10	40	46	22
Accrington	22	6	8	8	48	48	20
Everton	22	9	2	11	35	46	20
Burnley	22	7	3	12	42	62	17
Derby County	22	7	2	13	41	61	16
NOTTS COUNTY	22	5	2	15	40	73	12
Stoke City	22	4	4	14	26	51	12

FIRST TEAM – SORT OF!

Records no longer exist for County's first reported friendly against Trent Valley on 8 December 1864 at the Meadows Cricket Ground. The score was 0–0 and just under a month later, the 'Pies took on Sheffield – and the starting line-up was recorded for posterity. Sheffield won 1–0 and the group, which seemed to include several siblings, was:

J. Patterson (captain), T. Elliott, W. Elliott, R. Fountain, R. Daft, C. Daft, G. Parr, John Parr, H. Parr, J.W. Thackery, J.B. Gibson, E.B. Stegman, A. Scrimshaw, W. Goddard, H. Simons, J.S. Wright, W. Wright

FIRST RECORDED GOAL

It was after almost a year of playing friendlies – four in all – before G. Packer broke the club's duck with a goal in the 2–1 defeat to – who else? – Sheffield.

FIRST FA CUP TIE

Old adversaries Sheffield were County's first FA Cup opponents with an estimated crowd of 1,500 watching a 1–1 draw at Trent Bridge on 3 November 1877 with Harry Cursham scoring the club's first official goal. The Yorkshiremen won the replay 3–0.

FIRST LEAGUE GAME

The 2–1 defeat to Everton on 15 September 1888 was County's first league game and Albert Moore had the distinction of scoring the club's first league goal, though the defeat somewhat blemished the occasion.

FIRST LEAGUE CUP TIE

Brighton & Hove Albion left Meadow Lane victorious after a 3–1 win in County's first League Cup tie. Harry Noon scored the hosts' goal – his only strike in 131 games for the club.

BYE-BYE CLOUGHIE

County took part in a Brian Clough farewell at the end of the 1992/93 campaign. The man who had turned Forest into a major force in England was finally stepping down and the match at the City Ground attracted a gate of 12,493 fans. Forest won the game 3–0.

(YET MORE) SEQUENCES

Quick on the draw
County set a new record of drawn games when they managed six on the bounce during the 2008/09 campaign. The club had three consecutive 0–0 draws during the 1984/85 season and in 1959/60, the 'Pies went 22 games without drawing a single game.

Goals

County bagged a record 107 goals during the 1959/60 campaign. The Magpies scored four goals on seven occasions, five goals in three matches, seven once and scored in their last 31 games of the campaign. All in all, a pleasant season.

Home sweet home

On only one occasion have the Magpies remained unbeaten at home for an entire season. In 1970/71 County won 19 and drew 4 of their 23 Meadow Lane fixtures on their way to winning the Division Four title.

AWAY THE LADS!

County were on fire on the road during the 1997/98 season, winning no less than 15 times away from Meadow Lane on their way to the fourth-tier title. County racked up 99 points during a memorable campaign and a particularly happy one for the delirious band of travelling fans.

PENALTY SHOOT-OUTS

County have been involved in ten penalty shoot-outs over the years with varying degrees of success, winning on six occasions and losing the other four. Here is the breakdown, including the competitions the matches fell under:

6 October 2009   Football League Trophy
Lost 3–2 v Bradford City

12 August 2003   League Cup
Won 7–6 v Preston North End

15 October 2003   Football League Trophy
Lost 4–2 v Barnsley

15 December 1998   FA Cup
Won 4–2 v Wigan Athletic

28 January 1997   Football League Trophy
Lost 4–2 v Scunthorpe Utd

31 January 1995   Anglo-Italian Cup
Won 3–2 v Stoke City to reach final

16 February 1994   Anglo-Italian Cup
Won 4–3 v Southend Utd to reach final

22 October 1991   Full Members' Cup
Won 2–1 v Sheffield United

11 December 1990   Full Members' Cup
Lost 5–3 v Sunderland

21 February 1990   Associate Members' Cup
Won 4–3 v Hereford Utd

TWENTY QUESTIONS:
TOMMY LAWTON

1   Tommy was born in Farnworth near Bolton on
    6 October 1919.

2   Tommy began to score goals for his school and
    junior side Hayes Athletic, finding the net 570
    times over a three-year period.

3   Due to his flat feet, Tommy had to wear specially
    designed boots.

4   Tommy joined Burnley from school and stayed with
    the Clarets for one season, making his first-team
    debut aged 16 years and 174 days old – the youngest
    centre-forward ever to play league football.

5   Everton paid the princely sum of £6,500 for him and
    paired him alongside legendary striker Dixie Dean
    for a time.

6   During the Second World War, Tommy served as
    a physical training instructor and guested for
    Chester and Greenock Morton.

7   Like so many of his generation, he was robbed of his
    best years by the war, but in that time he scored
    152 goals in 114 games, though none of those
    counted towards his final career stats.

8   Tommy scored 24 goals in 23 wartime internationals
    for England.

9   After the war, Tommy signed for Chelsea for
    £11,500 but didn't take to life in London and
    demanded a transfer.

10 Lawton shocked the football world by joining third-tier side Notts County in 1947 for £20,000 and became an instant crowd idol at Meadow Lane, helping draw massive crowds and inspiring the club to promotion.

11 Tommy won 23 caps for England, scoring 22 times.

12 He left for a player/manager role at Brentford on 1952.

13 Tommy appeared in a film, *The Great Game*, in 1952.

14 He finished his career with Arsenal before retiring in 1955.

15 Tommy later became player/manager at Kettering before returning to manage, briefly, at County, though his spell was something of a disappointment.

16 In 1954 Lawton published the book, *Soccer the Lawton Way*. This was followed by *My Twenty Years of Soccer* (1955).

17 Tommy was married twice and has one son and one daughter.

18 In later years he became a columnist for the *Nottingham Evening Post*.

19 After Lawton fell on hard times, Everton awarded him a testimonial in 1972.

20 Tommy Lawton died in Nottingham on 6 November 1996.

RANDOM QUOTES

'I think it was probably the best goal I've scored. The most important anyway. The cross from Dean Thomas bulleted towards me and I got my shape right early. It then flew off my boot.'

Mark Draper on his wonder strike against Sunderland in 1993

'I think there might be repercussions from being a Midlands club in the division. There are so many from this patch. It points the way to a battle every time we play each other. We're ready for one next Saturday at Peterborough. If I were the manager, say, of a southern First Division team I would be pleased to see so many Midlands clubs.'

Neil Warnock laments the abundance of second-tier clubs within kicking distance of Nottingham, 1992

'It's the best result since I took over as Notts manager . . . though I wouldn't say the performance was outstanding. It was the best result because of the satisfaction derived from the fact we've been the city's underdogs for many years.'

Mick Walker after a satisfying 2–1 win over Forest in 1994

ANGLO-SCOTTISH CUP

County have taken part in the Anglo-Scottish Cup on four different occasions, failing to win the tournament which pitted English teams against each other in the first phase of matches before the battle with the clubs north of the border commenced. County's first opponents were Brian Clough's Nottingham Forest in August 1976 – you can't get much closer than that for an international tournament – when the two rivals fought out a 0–0 draw at Meadow Lane. Away defeats to Bristol City and West Brom put paid to Jimmy Sirrel's side's hopes – at least for that season. However, County came back for more punishment the following season and came within a hair's breadth of going all the way to the final.

After beating Hull City 1–0 at Meadow Lane in front of 4,020 curious locals, a 0–0 draw at Oldham Athletic was followed by a 5–4 win at Sheffield United. Oddly, despite County earning more group points, goals meant bonus points and that led to a play-off with Sheffield United who were soundly beaten 3–0 in Nottingham with the hosts progressing to the quarter-finals. Motherwell were the first Scottish opponents faced and after a 1–1 draw at Fir Park, County edged past the 'Well 1–0 at Meadow Lane. The Magpies fans were hardly enamoured by the competition, and just 5,384 came to see the semi-final first leg against St Mirren in which Arthur Mann scored the only goal. The Scots won the second leg 2–0 at Love Street to go on to the final where they lost to Bristol City.

Two wins out of three in the group stages of the 1978/79 competition was not enough to progress further and the 1979/80 effort also ended at the first hurdle. The final year of the tournament, the 1980/81 season, saw County go all the way to the final. County won one and drew two of their three group matches to finish top of the table and face Morton in the next round. A 2–0 home win and a 1–1 draw in Scotland saw Notts take on Kilmarnock in the semi-final and after winning the away leg 2–1, County strolled into the final with a 5–2 second-leg win. With Chesterfield waiting in the final, County lost 1–0 at Saltergate in the first leg, watched by 10,190 fans, but despite almost 13,000 turning out to cheer on the lads at Meadow Lane, the Spireites held out for a 1–1 draw to lift the cup.

Total record in the Anglo-Scottish Cup:

P	W	D	L	F	A
26	12	7	7	35	29

HAVANT A CLUE?

County's most embarrassing loss was the December 2007 FA Cup second round home defeat to non-league Havant & Waterlooville. The visitors scored the only goal while two divisions below their League Two hosts.

CLUB FACTS & HONOURS

First Football League game: 15 September 1888 v Everton (a) Lost 2–1

Highest Home Attendance: 47,310 v York City, 12 March 1955 in FA Cup 6th Round

Lowest Home Attendance: 1,927 v Chesterfield, 11 February 1967 in Division 4

Best League Win: 11–1 v Newport County, 15 January 1949 in Division 3 (South)

Best Cup Win: 15–0 v Rotherham, 24 October 1885 in FA Cup 1st Round

Worst League Defeat: 1–9 v Aston Villa, 29 September 1888 in Division 1
1–9 v Blackburn Rovers, 16 November 1889 in Division 1
1–9 v Portsmouth, 9 April 1927 in Division 2

Most League Points (2 points for a win): 69 in Divison 4, 1970/71

Most League Points (3 points for a win): 99 in Division 3, 1997/98

Most League Goals: 107 in Division 4, 1959/60

Most Capped Player: Kevin Wilson (15 caps for Northern Ireland)

Most League Appearances: Albert Iremonger, 564

Most League Goals: Les Bradd, 124

Most Goals in a Season: Tom Keetley, 39 in 1930/31

FA Cup Winners: 1894

Anglo-Italian Cup winners: 1995

Division 1 Winners: Never

Division 2 Winners: 1896/97, 1913/14, 1922/23

Division 3 Winners: 1930/31 (Div 3 S), 1949/50 (Div 3 S), 1997/98

Division 4 Winners: 1970/71

Championship Winners: Never

Premiership Winners: Never

League One Winners: Never

League Two Winners: 2009/10

Highest Transfer Fee Received: £2,500,000 for Craig Short to Derby County, September 1992

Highest Transfer Fee Paid: £685,000 for Tony Agana to Sheffield United, November 1991

SHORT AND SWEET

Steve Cotterill was one of the club's most successful managers – despite his brief stay in the Meadow Lane hot-seat. Here are a few of the pearls of wisdom which he shared during his time as the boss:

'I've been quite lucky in my managerial career in that I've had a few highs, and not too many downs. This one would be a good achievement. How good is still to be measured.'

'We want to keep our heads down. We're not going to be shouting from the roof-tops about where we are because this game quite often comes back to kick you in the teeth.'

'It's a measure of how well the players have done and we're delighted with how they have applied themselves. They have been nothing short of magnificent.'

IF THE CAP FITS ...

County have never had a player who has won bundles of international caps while with the club. The player who holds the 'most-capped' record is striker Kevin Wilson, who won 15 for Northern Ireland during his time at Meadow Lane. Wilson made 69 appearances at Notts County, scoring three goals between 1991 and 1993.

JOBSWORTHS

There aren't many players who have had surnames that are also jobs, of sorts. Our research shows there to have been just five so far – and here they are ...

Barber, Mike	1963–5
Butler, Peter	1994–5
Friars, Emmet	2004–6
King, Phil	1993–4
Marshall, Shaun	2005–6

PLAY-OFFS

The Magpies' first attempt at promotion via the play-offs was in 1987/88 when a 4th-place finish in Division Three set up a semi-final with Walsall, but a 3–1 first-leg defeat at Meadow Lane swayed the balance the Saddlers' way and a 1–1 draw in the second leg resulted in a 4–2 aggregate defeat.

In 1989/90, County went one better, drawing with Bolton away and then beating them 2–0 at a packed Meadow Lane. That meant a Wembley final against Tranmere and, winning their first final at the famous old stadium, goals from Tommy Johnson and Craig Short gave Neil Warnock's side a 2–0 win in front of almost 30,000 fans.

The 'Pies secured their second successive promotion the year after when, having seen off Middlesbrough in the semi-final (1–1 away and 1–0 at home), they went on to face Brighton & Hove Albion at Wembley for the right to play in the top flight. Almost 60,000 witnessed County win 3–1 with a double from Tommy Johnson and another from Dave Regis enough on the day.

The last time County made it to a play-off final, things weren't so enjoyable. Having beaten Crewe Alexandra over two legs for the right to promotion to Division One (now the Championship), they faced Bradford City at Wembley Stadium in front of just shy of 40,000, but the Bantams, who had finished two places lower in the table than County, triumphed 2–0. Rough justice, some might say, but those are the rules . . .

TOMMY LAWTON QUOTES

'I had never been able to kick a ball with my left foot, but every afternoon at four o'clock after school, he took me across to the field and we practised shooting and passing with a plimsoll on my right foot and a boot on my left. He would kick the ball across to me and I had to shoot from whatever angle.'

Tommy on influential schoolmaster Bunny Lee

'We made goalposts with coats and jackets and we'd just play any time of the day.'

Tommy on the halcyon days of 'jumpers for goalposts'

'On Sunday mornings, after church, there was usually a game organised against a team from another part of Bolton with side stakes. We would get a tanner a man if you were on the winning side. . . A tanner, you see, paid for their Saturday night out, a couple of pints and a packet of fags.'

Tommy on his early pay (and fag) packets as a youngster

'He was my staunchest admirer and pal, he nursed and advised me. He was one of the main reasons why I was able to get such a great start in football.'

Tommy on his influential grandfather James Riley

'I never was capped at schoolboy level. I cannot understand why not. It was one of the biggest disappointments of my life.'

Tommy, a prolific scorer as a schoolboy was, for some reason, never recognised by England as a kid – something that clearly stayed with him all his life

'All they ever said was make sure you pass it to a man in the same shirt.'

Tommy on the simple advice the older Everton players gave him

'The next time we both went for a cross, I end up on the ground with blood streaming from my nose. Wilf was looking down at me and he said "Ah told thee, Tom. Tha's jumping too high!" My nose was broken. When Arsenal came to Everton, Copping broke my nose again! He was hard, Wilf. You always had something to remember him by when you played against him.'

Tommy on the pummelling he took from Arsenal's hard-as-nails defender Wilf Copping

'I remember my first meeting with Hughie Gallacher. It was after I had had a bad game for Burnley Reserves against Derby County Reserves. I was walking off the pitch with my heart in my boots when Hughie, who was the Derby centre-forward, came up to me and said, "Look, son, you must learn to cover the ball with your body. If you are being tackled on your right, keep the ball on your left foot, so your opponent will have to come across you to get at it, and it's the same the other way round. If you do that they won't take it from you." I shall never forget the great Hughie Gallacher for that.'

Tommy on perhaps the most important piece of career advice he ever received

THE WISDOM OF WARNOCK

Former County boss Neil Warnock dragged the Magpies from the depths of the third tier back to the top flight in successive seasons. One thing the former gaffer wasn't short of was good quotes . . .

'Craig Short was tremendous and, if I could have done, I would have liked to have given him 11 out of 10. He marked David Hirst in the first half and Trevor Francis in the second with equal distinction.'

Quintessential Warnock

'Harding marked John Sheridan out of the game and if I detailed him to mark the corner flag he would come out with flying colours.'

The boss, considering giving Phil Harding easier assignments

'Kevin Bartlett gets more criticism from the supporters than anybody, but he continues to create so many chances. If he could finish like Trevor Francis he would score 45 goals a season, and if Francis had still got Bartlett's legs we would have a multi-million pound Colossus between them.'

Imagine a 45-goal-a-season Colossus with Trevor Francis' body and Kevin Bartlett's legs – scary!

'It was a marvellous advert for the FA Cup, full of end-to-end excitement. Though goalkeeper Steve Cherry had a great game for us, I felt we had more chances than City, something not conveyed by BBC television's *Match of the Day*. We hadn't had a kick on grass since the league match at Portsmouth two weeks earlier, and it was only on Friday that we were able to go through our set-piece routine – on several inches of snow on the training ground . . . without a ball!'

Warnock celebrates the 1991 FA Cup win over Man City with typical enthusiasm

OUTGUNNED!

Few teams can claim to have a record that is at least on a par with Arsenal over the years. The Gunners' success over a sustained period means they inevitably have better records in head-to-heads against the majority of clubs, but that doesn't extend to the 'Pies. There haven't been that many meetings in recent years, but overall, Arsenal have come out second-best in meetings. Here is the complete record, up to the beginning of the 2010/11 season:

P: 46   W: 20   D: 7   L: 19   F: 67   A: 69

CLUB LEGENDS:
TOMMY JOHNSON (1988–91)

Appearances:	149
Goals:	57
Date of Birth:	15 January 1971
Birthplace:	Newcastle

Tommy Johnson made his Notts County debut aged just 17 after coming on as a substitute at home to Preston North End in September 1988. The game ended 0–0 but the youngster had done enough in the reserves and at youth level to merit his senior debut.

The teenager made a few more appearances as a substitute before gradually easing his way into the starting line-up before the end of the season. He restored his manager's faith by scoring twice for County in a 3–0 win over Huddersfield Town – it was only his second league start. Johnson scored twice more to end his first season with 4 goals from a total of 10 appearances and from then on, he was pretty much a first-team regular.

Boss Neil Warnock was convinced that Johnson could save him a small fortune in the transfer market and partnered him with the experienced Gary Lund for the 1988/89 campaign with impressive results. Johnson finished with 20 goals and scored vital goals in the play-offs to help the Magpies win promotion to Division Two.

Johnson was again a key figure in the 'Pies' second successive promotion the following season, scoring 21 goals and again managing to score in the play-off final – twice this time – as Warnock's side returned to the top flight for the first time.

By now Johnson had become a huge crowd favourite and despite several top clubs sniffing around the youngster, he remained a County player for one more season and though he would again finish the club's top scorer, the fairytale ended with a falling out with the manager and relegation for the Magpies.

Johnson joined Derby County for £1.3m in March 1992 and had spells with Aston Villa, Everton and Celtic at his peak. Later he played for Sheffield Wednesday, Kilmarnock and Gillingham. Few would argue, however, Johnson's best days were spent at Meadow Lane where, for a while, he had the world at his feet.

CLUB LEGENDS:
STEVE CHERRY (1989–95)

Appearances:	328
Goals:	0
Date of Birth:	5 August 1960
Birthplace:	Nottingham

Steve Cherry began his career down the road from Meadow Lane with Derby County, making 90 starts for the Rams during his time with the club. He then moved to Watford and later Plymouth Argyle before he finally found his way 'home' to Nottingham with the Magpies. By the time he arrived, Cherry had become one of the most coveted goalkeepers in the lower leagues and had been voted Player of the Year at both Derby and Plymouth.

He made his debut in February 1989 during a 1–0 loss to Chester City, replacing the long-serving Mick Leonard in the process. Cherry started all but one of the final 18 games of the season, and was an ever-present and started all 59 league and cup matches in the following campaign. He played a vital role in County's successive promotions back to the top and he became a huge favourite with Magpies fans with his consistently brilliant displays, which added a new dimension to the club's defence.

Despite relegation in his third full campaign, Cherry was again outstanding and played every match of County's ultimately disappointing 1991/92 season. After 170 consecutive games, Cherry finally missed a game three matches into the 1992/93 season, though was soon back between the sticks at Meadow Lane.

Reliable and rarely injured, Cherry was again inspirational throughout the 1993/94 season in which he missed just one game and was quite brilliant during the play-off semi-finals against Southend United.

His final season with the Magpies ended with relegation to Division Two and Cherry played in 33 league and cup games before being released at the end of the season. Following his release he had spells with two of his former clubs – Watford and Plymouth Argyle – as well as Rotherham United, Rushden & Diamonds, Mansfield Town, Oldham Athletic and Lincoln City, before hanging up his gloves at the age of 43. In 2010 he was goalkeeping coach with the League Two side Macclesfield Town.

THEY SAID IT ...

'I am rather calm about it. I have no problems with it. I just focus on the football and leave the other things to Peter Trembling. What can you do about it? I just take it easy.'

Hans Backe, a couple of days before he quit Meadow Lane for New York Red Bulls

'Sven is the main guy here. We still look at him like he's the England manager. He came in after this game and said we had done well and should be proud of ourselves. If he was to leave it would be a huge loss. I don't know what would happen to the club.'

Lee Hughes, but we'll get over it

'We have to get players in, but this team has done ever so well. The players we have kept are the ones we wanted to keep. They did so well last season. We need some additions but they have to be better than the players we have got. However, I am not going to disrupt things too much because these players deserve a chance. They had a record number of clean sheets and scored a record number of goals. The good thing is we have momentum and we have to keep that going. Team spirit is a big thing and you do not want to bring people in who are going to undermine that.'

Craig Short

'We've struggled in the last few years. But now, who knows? Before Sven we were 33-1 for the League Two title; now we're 7-1. Mind you, I won't be having a bet. This is Notts County ...'

NCFC matchday steward

'You're only here for the money!'

The ever-witty Forest fans serenade Sven at his first Notts County match

'The media frenzy will settle down. Sven will give me advice, I'll give him advice: that's how it will work.'

Ian McParland

NOTTS COUNTY: THE STATS

Chances are if you're looking for a particular record or season in the 'Pies history, you'll find it in the following pages . . .

MANAGERS

County have had an incredible 52 managers in total – compare that to Liverpool who've had just 18! Perhaps the revolving-door aspect of the hot seat at Meadow Lane has been partly responsible for the club's lack of success over the years. Here, with a complete listing of each boss, is a definitive record of the men who tried to make this football club great, with varying degrees of success! The last two columns indicate relegation and promotion.

From	To	P	W	D	L	R	P
Craig Short							
4-6-10	-	-	-	-	-	-	-
Steve Cotterill							
23-2-10	27-5-10	18	14	3	1	0	1

From	To	P	W	D	L	R	P
Dave Kevan (caretaker)							
15-12-09	23-2-10	11	6	3	2	0	0
Hans Backe							
27-10-09	15-12-09	11	5	4	2	0	0
Michael Johnson/							
Dave Kevan (caretaker)							
13-10-09	27-10-09	2	1	1	0	0	0
Ian McParland							
18-10-07	12-10-09	103	28	32	43	0	0
Steve Thompson							
12-6-06	16-10-07	65	21	25	19	0	0
Gudjon Thordarson							
17-5-05	26-5-06	50	14	21	19	0	0
Ian Richardson							
4-11-04	17-5-05	30	9	8	13	0	0
Gary Mills							
7-1-04	04-11-04	37	9	11	17	1	0
Bill Dearden							
07-1-02	07-1-04	92	26	25	41	0	0
Gary Brazil							
10-10-01	07-1-02	50	13	14	23	0	0
Jocky Scott							
28-6-2000	10-10-01	57	23	15	19	0	0

From	To	P	W	D	L	R	P
Sam Allardyce							
16-1-97	14-10-99	123	51	32	40	1	1
C. Murphy/							
S. Thompson							
5-6-95	23-12-96	72	27	22	23	1	0
Steve Nicol							
1-4-95	5-6-95	7	1	3	3	1	0
Howard Kendall							
12-1-95	1-4-95	14	4	4	6	1	0
Russell Slade							
15-9-94	12-1-95	18	3	4	11	1	0
Mick Walker							
14-1-93	14-9-94	75	29	18	28	1	0
Neil Warnock							
5-1-89	14-1-93	189	79	48	62	1	2
John Barnwell							
7-6-87	2-12-88	64	25	21	18	0	0
Jimmy Sirrel							
1-5-85	31-5-87	99	43	29	27	1	0
Richie Barker							
5-11-84	19-4-85	24	5	5	14	1	0
Larry Lloyd							
7-7-83	21-10-84	53	12	11	30	2	0

	From	To	P	W	D	L	R	P
Howard Wilkinson	1-7-82	30-6-83	42	15	7	20	0	0
Jimmy Sirrel	5-10-78	1-7-82	201	67	68	66	0	1
Ron Fenton	1-11-75	5-10-77	82	32	22	28	0	0
Jimmy Sirrel	1-11-69	15-10-75	267	127	70	70	0	2
Billy Gray	1-9-67	1-9-68	61	19	14	28	0	0
Andy Beattie	1-2-67	1-9-67	33	10	9	14	0	0
Jack Burkitt	1-4-66	1-2-67	35	12	8	15	0	0
Tim Coleman	12-4-65	18-3-66	18	7	5	6	0	0
Eddie Lowe	1-7-63	12-4-65	87	22	21	44	1	0
Tim Coleman	31-10-61	31-6-63	75	30	19	26	0	0
Frank Hill	17-10-58	31-10-61	140	59	27	54	1	1

From	To	P	W	D	L	R	P
Tommy Lawton							
7-5-57	1-7-58	42	12	6	24	1	0
George Poyser							
22-10-53	7-1-57	137	46	30	61	0	0
Eric Houghton							
25-5-49	1-9-53	173	70	37	66	0	1
Arthur Stollery							
12-6-46	15-2-49	112	47	22	43	0	0
Frank Buckley							
1-3-44	11-5-46						
Frank Womack		All three managed					
14-7-42	04-11-43	during the Second					
		World War – official					
Tony Towers		records are not					
13-7-39	14-7-42	available					
Harry Parkes							
11-1-38	13-7-39	62	22	13	27	0	0
Jimmy McMullan							
10-11-36	29-12-37	49	29	10	10	0	0
Percy Smith							
1-7-35	31-10-36	58	20	22	16	0	0
David Pratt							
1-4-35	1-6-35	1	0	0	1	1	0

	From	To	P	W	D	L	R	P
Charlie Jones								
	1-5-34	1-12-34	61	15	13	33	1	0
Horace Henshall								
	1-8-27	1-5-34	294	105	80	109	1	1
Albert Fisher								
	1-8-13	31-5-27	412	155	104	153	2	2
Tom Harris								
	1-8-1893	31-5-1913	N/A					
Tom Featherstone								
	1-1-93	31-05-93	N/A					
Edwin Browne								
	1-8-83	31-5-93	N/A					

FINAL PLACINGS

Here is a complete list of all County's final league positions since 1864:

2009/10	League Two	1st
2008/09	League Two	19th
2007/08	League Two	21st
2006/07	League Two	13th
2005/06	League Two	21st
2004/05	League Two	19th
2003/04	Division Two	23rd
2002/03	Division Two	15th
2001/02	Division Two	19th

2000/01	Division Two	8th
1999/2000	Division Two	8th
1998/99	Division Two	16th
1997/98	Division Three	1st
1996/97	Division Two	24th
1995/96	Division Two	4th
1994/95	Division One	24th
1993/94	Division One	7th
1992/93	Division One	17th
1991/92	Division One	21st
1990/91	Division Two	4th
1989/90	Division Three	3rd
1988/89	Division Three	9th
1987/88	Division Three	4th
1986/87	Division Three	7th
1985/86	Division Three	8th
1984/85	Division Two	20th
1983/84	Division One	21st
1982/83	Division One	15th
1981/82	Division One	15th
1980/81	Division Two	2nd
1979/80	Division Two	17th
1978/79	Division Two	6th
1977/78	Division Two	15th
1976/77	Division Two	8th
1975/76	Division Two	5th
1974/75	Division Two	14th
1973/74	Division Two	10th
1972/73	Division Three	2nd
1971/72	Division Three	4th
1970/71	Division Four	1st
1969/70	Division Four	7th
1968/69	Division Four	19th
1967/68	Division Four	17th
1966/67	Division Four	20th

1965/66	Division Four	8th
1964/65	Division Four	13th
1963/64	Division Three	24th
1962/63	Division Three	7th
1961/62	Division Three	13th
1960/61	Division Three	5th
1959/60	Division Four	2nd
1958/59	Division Three	23rd
1957/58	Division Two	21st
1956/57	Division Two	20th
1955/56	Division Two	20th
1954/55	Division Two	7th
1953/54	Division Two	14th
1952/53	Division Two	19th
1951/52	Division Two	15th
1950/51	Division Two	17th
1949/50	Division Three South	1st
1948/49	Division Three South	11th
1947/48	Division Three South	6th
1946/47	Division Three South	12th
1939–46	*No League due to Second World War*	
1938/39	Division Three South	11th
1937/38	Division Three South	11th
1936/37	Division Three South	2nd
1935/36	Division Three South	9th
1934/35	Division Two	22nd
1933/34	Division Two	18th
1932/33	Division Two	15th
1931/32	Division Two	16th
1930/31	Division Three South	1st
1929/30	Division Two	22nd
1928/29	Division Two	5th
1927/28	Division Two	15th
1926/27	Division Two	16th
1925/26	Division One	22nd

1924/25	Division One	9th
1923/24	Division One	10th
1922/23	Division Two	1st
1921/22	Division Two	13th
1920/21	Division Two	6th
1919/20	Division One	21st
1915–19	*No League due to First World War*	
1914/15	Division One	16th
1913/14	Division Two	1st
1912/13	Division One	19th
1911/12	Division One	16th
1910/11	Division One	11th
1909/10	Division One	9th
1908/09	Division One	15th
1907/08	Division One	18th
1906/07	Division One	18th
1905/06	Division One	16th
1904/05	Division One	18th
1903/04	Division One	13th
1902/03	Division One	15th
1901/02	Division One	13th
1900/01	Division One	3rd
1899/00	Division One	15th
1898/99	Division One	5th
1897/98	Division One	13th
1896/97	Division Two	1st
1895/96	Division Two	10th
1894/95	Division Two	2nd
1893/94	Division Two	3rd
1892/93	Division One	14th
1891/92	Football League	8th
1890/91	Football League	3rd
1889/90	Football League	10th
1888/89	Football League	11th
Until 1889/89	No League existed	

DERBY DAY

County versus Nottingham Forest is one of the world's oldest derby games and it's Forest who slightly hold the edge overall (boo!). In the 139 meetings up to the 2009/10 season, Forest had won 52 compared to County's 42, while 45 had ended in a draw. Below are all the stats any anorak could ever wish for regarding this famous old fixture.

12 February 1994	County 2–1 Forest	Division One (new)
30 October 1993	Forest 1–0 County	Division One (new)
15 September 1993	Forest 1–1 County	Anglo-Italian Cup
11 January 1992	Forest 1 –1 County	First Division
24 August 1991	County 0–4 Forest	First Division
31 March 1984	County 0–0 Forest	First Division
16 October 1983	Forest 3–1 County	First Division
23 April 1983	Forest 2–1 County	First Division
4 December 1982	County 3–2 Forest	First Division
12 April 1982	County 1–2 Forest	First Division
23 January 1982	Forest 0–2 County	First Division
25 October 1977	Forest 4–0 County	League Cup
9 April 1977	County 1–1 Forest	Second Division
8 March 1977	Forest 1–2 County	Second Division
7 August 1976	County 0–0 Forest	Anglo-Scottish Cup
13 April 1976	County 0–0 Forest	Second Division
30 August 1975	Forest 0–1 County	Second Division
25 March 1975	County 2–2 Forest	Second Division
28 December 1974	Forest 0–2 County	Second Division
3 March 1974	Forest 0–0 County	Second Division
26 December 1973	County 0–1 Forest	Second Division

1 May 1957	Forest 2–4 County	Second Division
20 October 1956	County 1–2 Forest	Second Division
11 February 1956	County 1–3 Forest	Second Division
1 October 1955	Forest 0–2 County	Second Division
12 February 1955	County 4–1 Forest	Second Division
25 September 1954	Forest 0–1 County	Second Division
27 February 1954	County 1–1 Forest	Second Division
10 October 1953	Forest 5–0 County	Second Division
3 January 1953	Forest 1–0 County	Second Division
30 August 1952	County 3–2 Forest	Second Division
19 January 1952	Forest 3–2 County	Second Division
15 September 1951	County 2–2 Forest	Second Division
22 April 1950	County 2–0 Forest	Third Division (South)
3 December 1949	Forest 1–2 County	Third Division (South)
9 February 1935	Forest 2–3 County	Second Division
29 September 1934	County 3–5 Forest	Second Division
17 February 1934	County 1–0 Forest	Second Division
7 October 1933	Forest 2–0 County	Second Division
18 February 1933	Forest 3–0 County	Second Division
8 October 1932	County 2–4 Forest	Second Division
13 February 1932	County 2–6 Forest	Second Division
3 October 1931	Forest 2–1 County	Second Division
4 January 1930	County 0–0 Forest	Second Division
7 September 1929	Forest 1–1 County	Second Division
2 March 1929	Forest 1–2 County	Second Division
20 October 1928	County 1–1 Forest	Second Division
22 February 1928	County 1–2 Forest	Second Division
17 September 1927	Forest 2–1 County	Second Division
5 February 1927	Forest 2–0 County	Second Division
18 September 1926	County 1–2 Forest	Second Division
24 January 1925	Forest 0–0 County	First Division
20 September 1924	County 0–0 Forest	First Division
29 September 1923	Forest 1–0 County	First Division

22 September 1923	County 2–1 Forest	First Division
14 November 1921	Forest 0–0 County	Second Division
5 November 1921	County 1–1 Forest	Second Division
18 September 1920	County 2–0 Forest	Second Division
11 September 1920	Forest 1–0 County	Second Division
26 December 1913	Forest 1–0 County	Second Division
25 December 1913	County 2–2 Forest	Second Division
31 December 1910	Forest 2–0 County	First Division
3 September 1910	County 1–1 Forest	First Division
8 January 1910	County 4–1 Forest	First Division
4 September 1909	Forest 2–1 County	First Division
27 March 1909	Forest 1–0 County	First Division
21 November 1908	County 3–0 Forest	First Division
4 April 1908	County 2–0 Forest	First Division
7 December 1907	Forest 2–0 County	First Division
25 December 1905	Forest 1–2 County	First Division
4 November 1905	County 1–1 Forest	First Division
25 March 1905	County 1–2 Forest	First Division
26 November 1904	Forest 2–1 County	First Division
25 December 1903	Forest 0–1 County	First Division
28 November 1903	County 1–3 Forest	First Division
26 December 1902	County 1–1 Forest	First Division
15 November 1902	Forest 0–0 County	First Division
26 December 1901	Forest 1–0 County	First Division
16 November 1901	County 3–0 Forest	First Division
26 December 1900	County 1–0 Forest	First Division
24 October 1900	Forest 5–0 County	First Division
17 March 1900	Forest 0–3 County	First Division
11 November 1899	County 1–2 Forest	First Division
4 February 1899	Forest 0–0 County	First Division
8 October 1898	County 2–2 Forest	First Division
9 October 1897	County 1–3 Forest	First Division
4 September 1897	Forest 1–1 County	First Division
3 March 1894	County 4–1 Forest	FA Cup
24 February 1894	Forest 1–1 County	FA Cup

25 February 1893	Forest 3–1 County	First Division
8 October 1892	County 3–0 Forest	First Division
26 December 1891	County 0–1 Forest	Friendly
3 October 1891	Forest 3–1 County	Friendly
18 April 1891	Forest 2–4 County	Friendly
26 December 1890	County 0–0 Forest	Friendly
26 December 1889	County 1–1 Forest	Friendly
30 November 1889	Forest 2–4 County	Friendly
30 March 1889	Forest 2–5 County	Friendly
26 December 1888	County 4–1 Forest	Friendly
1 December 1888	Forest 3–0 County	Friendly
26 December 1887	County 0–0 Forest	Friendly
3 December 1887	Forest0–1 County	Friendly
26 November 1887	Forest 2–1 County	FA Cup
16 April 1887	Forest 3–1 County	Notts County Cup
19 March 1887	County 1–1 Forest	Notts County Cup
12 February 1887	Forest 1–2 County	Friendly
27 December 1886	County 0–2 Forest	Friendly
16 January 1886	County 5–0 Forest	Friendly
28 November 1885	Forest 1–4 County	Friendly
18 April 1885	County 3–2 Forest	Friendly
26 December 1884	County 0–3 Forest	Friendly
26 December 1883	County 5–1 Forest	Friendly
1 December 1883	County 3–0 Forest	FA Cup
20 October 1883	Forest 0–0 County	Friendly
20 January 1883	Forest 1–1 County	Friendly
11 February 1882	County 1–2 Forest	Friendly
17 December 1881	Forest 0–5 County	Friendly
5 March 1881	County 1–0 Forest	Friendly
16 October 1880	Forest 4–0 County	Friendly
17 January 1880	Forest 7–1 County	Friendly
8 November 1879	Forest 4–0 County	FA Cup
16 November 1878	County 1–3 Forest	FA Cup

8 February 1877	County 1–1 Forest	Friendly
18 November 1876	County 2–0 Forest	Friendly
29 February 1876	County 1–0 Forest	Friendly
13 November 1875	Forest 2–1 County	Friendly
14 November 1874	County 0–0 Forest	Friendly
7 February 1874	County 0–0 Forest	Friendly
27 December 1873	Forest 1–1 County	Friendly
4 January 1873	County 0–0 Forest	Friendly
7 December 1872	Forest 1–0 County	Friendly
26 February 1872	Forest 2–1 County	Friendly
14 February 1872	County 0–1 Forest	Friendly
11 March 1871	Forest 1–1 County	Friendly
6 November 1869	Forest 0–0 County	Friendly
28 February 1867	County 1–0 Forest	Friendly
13 December 1866	Forest 1–1 County	Friendly
19 April 1866	County 0–0 Forest	Friendly
22 March 1866	Forest 0–0 County	Friendly

FA CUP – COMPLETE RECORD

Here is County's complete FA Cup record, from the first game played in 1879, to the last tie played in 2010.

Season	Opp	Rnd	H/A	Score
2009/10	Fulham	5	A	0–4
	Wigan Athletic	4r	A	2–0
	Wigan Athletic	4	H	2–2
	Forest Green Rovers	3	H	2–1
	Bournemouth	2	A	2–1
	Bradford City	1	A	2–1
2008/09	Kettering Town	2r	A	1–2
	Kettering town	2	H	1–1
	Sutton Utd	1	A	1–0

Season	Opp	Rnd	H/A	Score
2007/08	Havant & Waterlooville	2	H	0–1
	Histon	1	H	3–0
2006/07	Leyton Orient	1	A	1–2
2005/06	Torquay Utd	2	A	1–2
	Bristol City	1	A	2–0
2004/05	Middlesbrough	3	H	1–2
	Swindon Town	2r	H	2–0
	Swindon Town	2	A	1–1
	Woking	1	H	2–0
2003/04	Middlesbrough	3	A	0–2
	Gravesend & Northfleet	2	A	2–1
	Shildon	1	H	7–2
2002/03	Southport	1	A	2–4
2001/02	Wycombe Wanderers	2	A	0–3
	Cambridge Utd	1r	H	2–0
	Cambridge Utd	1	A	1–1
2000/01	Wimbledon	3r	H	0–1 aet
	Wimbledon	3	A	2–2
	Wigan Athletic	2r	H	2–1 aet
	Wigan Athletic	2	A	1–1
	Gravesend & Northfleet	1	A	2–1
1999/2000	Bournemouth	1r	A	2–4
	Bournemouth	1	H	1–1
1998/99	Sheffield Utd	3r	H	3–4 aet
	Sheffield Utd	3	A	1–1
	Wigan Athletic	2r	A	0–0 aet
	Wigan Athletic	2	H	1–1
	Hendon	1r	H	3–0
	Hendon	1	A	0–0
1997/98	Preston	2r	H	1–2 aet
	Preston	2	A	2–2
	Colwyn Bay	1	H	2–0

Season	Opp	Rnd	H/A	Score
1996/97	Aston Villa	3r	A	0–3
	Aston Villa	3	H	0–0
	Rochdale	2	H	3–1
	Newcastle Town	1	A	2–0
1995/96	Middlesbrough	3	H	1–2
	Telford	2	A	2–0
	York City	1	A	1–0
1994/95	Manchester City	3r	A	2–5
	Manchester City	3	A	2–2
1993/94	West Ham	4r	A	0–1 aet
	West Ham	4	H	1–1
	Sutton Utd	3	H	3–2
1992/93	Sunderland	3	H	0–2
1991/92	Norwich City	5	A	0–3
	Blackburn Rovers	4	H	2–1
	Wigan Athletic	3	H	2–0
1990/91	Tottenham Hotspur	6	A	1–2
	Manchester City	5	H	1–0
	Oldham Athletic	4	H	2–0
	Hull City	3	A	5–2
1989/90	Doncaster Rovers	1	A	0–1
1988/89	Hartlepool Utd	2	A	0–1
	Darlington	1	A	2–1
1987/88	Port Vale	2	A	0–2
	Chesterfield	1r	A	1–0
	Chesterfield	1	H	3–3
1986/87	Middlesbrough	2	H	0–1
	Carlisle Utd	1r	A	3–0
	Carlisle Utd	1	H	1–1

Season	Opp	Rnd	H/A	Score
1985/86	Tottenham Hotspur	4r	A	0–5
	Tottenham Hotspur	4	H	1–1
	Stoke City	3	A	2–0
	Wrexham	2r	A	3–0
	Wrexham	2	H	2–2
	Scarborough	1	H	6–1
1984/85	Grimsby Town	3r	A	2–4
	Grimsby Town	3	H	2–2
1983/84	Everton	6	H	1–2
	Middlesbrough	5	H	1–0
	Huddersfield Town	4	A	2–1
	Bristol City	3r	A	2–0
	Bristol City	3	H	2–2
1982/83	Middlesbrough	4	A	0–2
	Leicester City	3	A	3–2
1981/82	Aston Villa	3	A	0–6
1980/81	Peterborough Utd	4	H	0–1
	Blackburn Rovers	3	H	2–1
1979/80	Wolves	3	H	1–3
1978/79	Arsenal	4	A	0–2
	Reading	3	H	4–2
1977/78	Millwall	5	A	1–2
	Brighton & HA	4	A	2–1
	Charlton Athletic	3	A	2–0
1976/77	Arsenal	3	H	0–1
1975/76	Leeds Utd	3	H	0–1
1974/75	QPR	4	A	0–3
	Portsmouth	3	H	3–1
1973/74	WBA	3	A	0–4
1972/73	Sunderland	3r	A	0–2
	Sunderland	3	H	1–1
	Lancaster City	2	H	2–1
	Altrincham	1	A	1–0

Season	Opp	Rnd	H/A	Score
1971/72	Derby County	4	A	0–6
	Watford	3	A	4–1
	South Shields (1936)	2	A	3–1
	Newport County	1	H	6–0
1970/71	Leicester City	3	A	0–2
	Bury	2r	H	3–0
	Bury	2	A	1–1
	Port Vale	1	H	1–0
1969/70	Rotherham Utd	1	H	0–3
1968/69	Doncaster Rovers	1	A	0–1
1967/68	Runcorn Halton	1	A	0–1
1966/67	Oldham Athletic	1	A	1–3
1965/66	Southend Utd	1	A	1–3
1964/65	Brentford	2	A	0–4
	Chelmsford City	1	H	2–0
1963/64	Doncaster Rovers	2r	H	1–2
	Doncaster Rovers	2	A	1–1
	Frickley Colliery	1	H	2–1
1962/63	Peterborough Utd	1	H	0–3
1961/62	Manchester City	3	H	0–1
	Margate	2r	H	3–1
	Margate	2	A	1–1
	Yeovil Town	1	H	4–2
1960/61	Aldershot	1	A	0–2
1959/60	Bath City	2	H	0–1
	Hastings Utd	1	A	2–1
1958/59	Barrow	1	H	0–1
1957/58	Bristol City	4	H	1–2
	Tranmere Rovers	3	H	2–0
1956/57	Rhyl	3	H	1–3
1955/56	Fulham	3	H	0–1

Season	Opp	Rnd	H/A	Score
1954/55	York City	6	H	0–1
	Chelsea	5	H	1–0
	Sheffield Wed	4r	H	1–0 aet
	Sheffield Wed	4	A	1–1
	Middlesbrough	3	A	4–1
1953/54	Everton	3	A	1–2
1952/53	Bolton Wanderers	4r2	N	0–1
	Bolton Wanderers	4r	H	2–2 aet
	Bolton Wanderers	4	A	1–1
	Leicester City	3	A	4–2
1951/52	Portsmouth	4	H	1–2
	Stockton	3	H	4–0
1950/51	Southampton	3	H	3–4
1949/50	Burnley	3	H	1–4
	Rochdale	2	A	2–1
	Tilbury	1	H	4–0
1948/49	Liverpool	4	A	0–1
	Plymouth Argyle	3	A	1–0 aet
	Barrow	2	H	3–2
	Port Vale	1	H	2–1
1947/48	Swindon Town	4	A	0–1
	Birmingham City	3	A	2–0
	Stockton	2r	A	4–1
	Stockton	2	H	1–1 aet
	Horsham	1	A	9–1
1946/47	Luton Town	3	A	0–6
	Swindon Town	2	H	2–1
	Leyton Orient	1	A	2–1
1945/46	Northampton Town	2 2l	H	1–0
	Northampton Town	2 1l	A	1–3
	Bradford City	1 2l	A	2–1
	Bradford City	1 1l	H	2–2

Season	Opp	Rnd	H/A	Score
1938/39	Walsall	4r	A	0–4
	Walsall	4	H	0–0
	Burnley	3	H	3–1
1937/38	Huddersfield Town	4	A	0–1
	Aldershot	3	A	3–1
1936/37	Gateshead AFC	1	A	0–2
1935/36	Tranmere Rovers	3r	A	3–4
	Tranmere Rovers	3	H	0–0
	Torquay Utd	2	H	3–0
	Grantham Town	1	A	2–0
1934/35	Wolves	3	A	0–4
1933/34	Swansea Town	3	A	0–1
1932/33	Tranmere Rovers	3	A	1–2
1931/32	Bristol City	3r	A	2–3
	Bristol City	3	H	2–2
1930/31	Sheffield Utd	4	A	1–4
	Swansea Town	3	H	3–1
	Doncaster Rovers	2	A	1–0
	Chesterfield	1	A	2–1
1929/30	West Ham Utd	3	A	0–4
1928/29	Derby County	3	A	3–4
1927/28	Sheffield Utd	3	H	2–3
1926/27	Newcastle Utd	3	A	1–8
1925/26	Fulham	5	H	0–1
	New Brighton	4	H	2–0
	Leicester City	3	H	2–0
1924/25	Cardiff City	3	H	0–2
	Norwich City	2	H	4–0
	Coventry City	1	A	2–0

Season	Opp	Rnd	H/A	Score
1923/24	Crystal Palace	2r3	N	1–2
	Crystal Palace	2r2	N	0–0 aet
	Crystal Palace	2r	H	0–0 aet
	Crystal Palace	2	A	0–0
	QPR	1	A	2–1
1922/23	Plymouth Argyle	1r	H	0–1
	Plymouth Argyle	1	A	0–0
1921/22	Huddersfield Town	sf	N	1–3
	Aston Villa	4r	A	4–3
	Aston Villa	4	H	2–2
	WBA	3r	H	2–0
	WBA	3	A	1–1
	Bradford City	2r2	N	1–0
	Bradford City	2r	H	0–0 aet
	Bradford City	2	A	1–1
	Grimsby Town	1r	H	3–0
	Grimsby Town	1	A	1–1
1920/21	Aston Villa	2r	A	0–1
	Aston Villa	2	H	1–1
	WBA	1	H	3–0
1919/20	Bradford Park Avenue	3	H	3–4
	Middlesbrough	2	H	1–0
	Millwall	1	H	2–0
1914/15	Bolton Wanderers	1	A	1–2
1913/14	Sheffield Wed	1	A	2–3
1912/13	Bristol Rovers	1	A	1–2
1911/12	Swindon Town	2	A	0–2
	Luton Town	1	A	4–2
1910/11	Swindon Town	1	A	1–3
1909/10	Bradford City	1	A	2–4
1908/09	Blackburn Rovers	1	H	0–1

Season	Opp	Rnd	H/A	Score
1907/08	Bolton Wanderers	2r	A	1–2 aet
	Bolton Wanderers	2	H	1–1
	Middlesbrough	1	H	2–0
1906/07	WBA	4	A	1–3
	Tottenham Hotspur	3	H	4–0
	Burslem PV	2r	H	5–0
	Burslem PV	2	A	2–2
	Preston North End	1	H	1–0
1905/06	Sunderland	1	A	0–1
1904/05	Bury	1	A	0–1
1903/04	Manchester Utd	1r	A	1–2
	Manchester Utd	1	H	3–3
1902/03	Bury	3	A	0–1
	Grimsby Town	2	A	2–0
	Southampton	1r2	N	2–1 aet
	Southampton	1r	A	2–2
	Southampton	1	H	0–0
1901/02	Reading	1	H	1–2
1900/01	Wolves	2	H	2–3
	Liverpool	1	H	2–0
1899/1900	Bury	2r	A	0–2
	Bury	2	H	0–0
	Chorley	1	H	6–0
1898/99	Southampton	2	H	0–1
	Kettering Town	1	H	2–0
1897/98	Wolves	1	H	0–1
1896/97	Aston Villa	2	A	1–2
	Small Heath	1	A	2–1
1895/96	Wolves	1r	H	3–4
	Wolves	1	A	2–2
1894/95	Sheffield Wed	1	A	1–5

Season	Opp	Rnd	H/A	Score
1893/94	Bolton Wanderers	f	N	4–1
	Blackburn Rovers	sf	N	1–0
	Nottingham Forest	3r	H	4–1
	Nottingham Forest	3	A	1–1
	Burton Wanderers	2	A	2–1
	Burnley	1	H	1–0
1892/93	Middlesbrough Iron.	2	A	2–3
	Shankhouse	1	H	4–0
1891/92	Sunderland	1r	A	0–4
	Sunderland	1	A	0–3
1890/91	Blackburn Rovers	f	N	1–3
	Sunderland	sfr	N	2–0
	Sunderland	sf	N	3–3
	Stoke City	3	H	1–0
	Burnley	2	H	2–1
	Sheffield Utd	1	A	9–1
1889/90	Sheffield Wed	3r2	N	1–2
	Sheffield Wed	3r	H	3–2
	Sheffield Wed	3	A	0–5
	Aston Villa	2	H	4–1
	Birmingham St Geo	1r	H	6–2
	Birmingham St Geo	1	A	4–4
1888/89	Sheffield Wed	2	A	2–3
	Old Brightonians	1	H	2–0
	Staveley	4q	A	3–1
	Derby Midland	3q	H	2–1
	Beeston St Johns	2q	H	4–2
	Eckington	1q	H	4–1
1887/88	Nottingham Forest	3	A	1–2
	Basford Rovers (scratched)			
	Lincoln Ramblers	1	H	9–0

Season	Opp	Rnd	H/A	Score
1886/87	WBA	6	H	1–2
	Marlow	5	H	5–2
	Bye	4		
	Staveley	3	A	3–0
	Notts Rangers	2r	A	5–0
	Notts Rangers	2	H	3–3
	Basford Rovers	1	H	13–0
1885/86	South Shore	5	A	1–2
	Bye	4		
	Notts Rangers	3	H	3–0
	Sheffield FC	2	H	8–0
	Rotherham Town	1	H	15–0
1884/85	Queens Park, Glasgow	6r	N	1–2
	Queens Park, Glasgow	6	H	2–2
	Bye	5		
	Walsall Swifts	4	A	4–0
	Sheffield FC	3	H	5–0
	Staveley	2	A	2–0
	Notts Olympic	1	H	2–0
1883/84	Blackburn Rovers	sf	N	0–1
	Swifts	5r	A	1–0
	Swifts	5	H	1–1 aet
	Bolton Wanderers	4r	A	2–1
	Bolton Wanderers	4	H	2–2
	Grantham Town	3	A	4–0
	Nottingham Forest	2	H	3–0
	Sheffield Heeley	1	H	3–1
1882/83	Old Etonians	sf	N	1–2
	Aston Villa	5	H	4–3
	Sheffield Wed	4	A	4–1
	Phoenix Bessemer	3	H	4–1
	Bye	2		
	Sheffield FC	1	H	6–1

Season	Opp	Rnd	H/A	Score
1881/82	Aston Villa	3r2	A	1–4
	Aston Villa	3r	H	2–2 aet
	Aston Villa	3	A	2–2
	Wednesbury Strollers	2r	H	11–1
	Wednesbury Strollers	2	H	5–3
				(match void)
	Walkover	1		
1880/81	Aston Villa	3	H	1–3
	Bye	2		
	Derbyshire FC	1r	A	4–2
	Derbyshire FC	1	H	4–4
1879/80	Nottingham Forest	1	A	0–4
1878/79	Nottingham Forest	1	H	1–3 aet
1877/78	Sheffield FC	1r	A	0–3
	Sheffield FC	1	H	1–1

LEAGUE CUP – COMPLETE RECORD

County's entire League Cup history is below:

Season	Rnd	Opp	H/A	Score
2009/10	1	Doncaster Rovers	H	0–1
2008/09	2	Wigan Athletic	A	0–4
	1	Doncaster Rovers	H	1–0
2007/08	1	Coventry City	A	0–3
2006/07	4	Wycombe Wanderers	H	0–1
	3	Southampton	H	2–0
	2	Middlesbrough	A	1–0
	1	Crystal Palace	A	2–1
2005/06	1	Watford	A	1–3
2004/05	2	West Ham Utd	A	2–3
	1	Bradford City	A	2–1

Season	Rnd	Opp	H/A	Score
2003/04	3	Chelsea	A	2–4
	2	Ipswich Town	H	2–1
	1	Preston NE	A	0–0
		(Notts County won 7–6 on penalties)		
2002/03	1	Oldham Athletic	A	2–3
2001/02	2	Manchester City	H	2–4
	1	Mansfield Town	A	4–3
2000/01	2	Watford	H	1–3
	2	Watford	A	2–0
		(aggregate 3–3, Watford won on away goals)		
	1	Hull City	H	2–0
	1	Hull City	A	0–1
1999/2000	2	Huddersfield Town	H	2–2
	2	Huddersfield Town	A	1–2
	1	Bury	H	2–0
	1	Bury	A	0–1
1998/99	1	Manchester City	H	0–2
	1	Manchester City	A	1–7
1997/98	2	Tranmere Rovers	H	0–2
	2	Tranmere Rovers	A	1–0
	1	Darlington	H	2–1
	1	Darlington	A	1–1
	2	Port Vale	H	3–2
		(aggregate 4–4, Port Vale won on away goals)		
1996/97	1	Bury	H	1–1
	1	Bury	A	0–1
1995/96	2	Leeds United	H	2–3
	2	Leeds United	A	0–0
	1	Lincoln City	H	2–0
	1	Lincoln City	A	2–0
1994/95	4	Norwich City	A	0–1
	3	Tottenham Hotspur	H	3–0
	2	Bristol City	H	3–0
	2	Bristol City	A	1–0

Season	Rnd	Opp	H/A	Score
1993/94	2	Newcastle Utd	H	1–7
	2	Newcastle Utd	A	1–4
	1	Hull City	H	2–0
	1	Hull City	A	1–3
(aggregate 3–3, Notts County won on away goals)				
1992/93	3	Cambridge Utd	H	2–3
	2	Wolves	H	3–2
	2	Wolves	A	1–0
1991/92	2	Port Vale	A	1–2
1990/91	2	Oldham Athletic	H	1–0
	2	Oldham Athletic	A	2–5
	1	Exeter City	H	1–0
	1	Exeter City	A	1–1
1989/90	1	Shrewsbury Town	H	3–1
	1	Shrewsbury Town	A	0–3
1988/89	2	Tottenham Hotspur	H	1–1
	2	Tottenham Hotspur	A	1–2
	1	Mansfield Town	H	5–0
	1	Mansfield Town	A	0–1
1987/88	1	Wolves	H	1–2
	1	Wolves	A	0–3
1986/87	1	Port Vale	H	1–3
	1	Port Vale	A	1–4
1985/86	2	Fulham	H	2–4
	2	Fulham	A	1–1
	1	Doncaster Rovers	H	1–0
	1	Doncaster Rovers	A	1–2
(aggregate 2–2, Notts County won on away goals)				
1984/85	4	Norwich City	A	0–3
	3	Bolton Wanderers	H	6–1
	2	Charlton Athletic	H	2–0
	2	Charlton Athletic	A	1–0

Season	Rnd	Opp	H/A	Score
1983/84	3r3	Birmingham City	H	1–3
	3r2	Birmingham City	A	0–0
	3r	Birmingham City	H	0–0
	3	Birmingham City	A	2–2
	2	Aldershot	H	4–1
	2	Aldershot	A	4–2
1982/83	4r	West Ham Utd	A	0–3
	4	West Ham Utd	H	3–3
	3	Chelsea	H	2–0
	2	Aston Villa	H	1–0
	2	Aston Villa	A	2–1
1981/82	2	Lincoln City	H	2–3
	2	Lincoln City	A	1–1
1980/81	4	Manchester City	A	1–5
	3	QPR	H	4–1
	2	Newport County	H	2–0
	2	Newport County	A	1–1
	1	Grimsby Town	H	3–0
	1	Grimsby Town	A	0–1
1979/80	3	Grimsby Town	A	1–3
	2	Torquay Utd	H	0–0
	2	Torquay Utd	A	1–0
1978/79	2	Crewe Alexandra	A	0–2
	1	Scunthorpe Utd	H	3–0
	1	Scunthorpe Utd	A	1–0
1977/78	3	Nottingham Forest	A	0–4
	2	Birmingham City	A	2–0
1976/77	3r	Derby County	H	1–2
	3	Derby County	A	1–1
	2	Scunthorpe Utd	A	2–0

Season	Rnd	Opp	H/A	Score
1975/76	qf	Newcastle United	A	0–1
	4r	Everton	H	2–0
	4	Everton	A	2–2
	3	Leeds Utd	A	1–0
	2	Sunderland	H	2–1
1974/75	2	Southampton	A	0–1
1973/74	1	Doncaster Rovers	H	3–4
1972/73	qf	Chelsea	A	1–3
	4	Stoke City	H	3–1
	3	Southampton	A	3–1
	2	Southport	H	3–2
	1	York City	H	3–1
1971/72	2	Gillingham	H	1–2
	1r	Leyton Orient	H	3–1
	1	Leyton Orient	A	1–1
1970/71	1	Aston Villa	A	0–4
1969/70	1	Mansfield Town	A	1–3
1968/69	1r	Grimsby Town	H	0–1
	1	Grimsby Town	A	0–0
1967/68	1	Rotherham Utd	H	0–1
1966/67	1r	Mansfield Town	A	0–3
	1	Mansfield Town	H	1–1
1965/66	1r	Chesterfield	A	1–2
	1	Chesterfield	H	0–0
1964/65	3	Chelsea	A	0–4
	2	Torquay Utd	A	2–1
	1	Newport County	H	3–2
1963/64	qf	Manchester City	H	0–1
	4	Portsmouth	H	3–2
	3	Bradford Park Avenue	H	3–2
	2	Blackburn Rovers	H	2–1

Season	Rnd	Opp	H/A	Score
1962/63	4	Birmingham City	A	2–3
	3	Swindon Town	H	5–0
	2	Southend Utd	A	3–2
1961/62	1r	Derby County	A	2–3
	1	Derby County	H	2–2
1960/61	2	Brighton & HA	H	1–3

ALL-TIME STATS

Up to the end of the 2009/10 season, County were the 15th-placed team in the all-time league table of England. This includes all games played (with wins, draws and losses, plus all the goals scored and conceded) to collate a list of who has been the most successful team in the country since league football began. Forest only made it to 19th (ha ha!)

County are the 34th most successful FA Cup team having played 320 games, winning 137 of their cup ties and drawing 61 times. The Magpies have been beaten on 122 occasions in the competition, scoring 584 goals and conceding 469.

In the League Cup, County are the 43rd-placed team in the all-time results table having played 139 ties and won 57 of them.

DIXIE LAND

The most prolific striker in history spent a short time with Notts County, though injuries meant his time at Meadow Lane was little more than a cameo role. Dixie

Dean arrived towards the back end of the 1937/38 season after his time at Everton finally came to a close. Though Dean's star was fading badly by the time he played for the Magpies, he was still a huge name in football and was welcomed by the County fans with open arms. But moving from the First Division to Division Three (South) must have been something of a culture shock for him, who made his debut during a 2–1 defeat at QPR. He played in the next two games, away to Gillingham and at home to Southend United, both of which ended in defeat, before his season was ended prematurely through injury. Although he missed the first game of the 1938/39 season, Dean played in the next three games and scored his first goals for the club, finding the net twice in a 5–1 win over Torquay United. He scored another against Newport before injury again kept him out of the team. He played his final game against Walsall on Bonfire Night 1938 – a drab 0–0 draw – before moving to Ireland to join Sligo Rovers. The odd fact of Dean's move to Nottingham is that a young pup had arrived at Goodison Park and effectively replaced him – the name? Future County legend Tommy Lawton!